Beneficial Barn Owls

The Entertaining Way to Rid Yourself of Rodents

Beneficial Barn Owls

The Entertaining Way to Rid Yourself of Rodents

Tom Stephan
Edited by Dorothy D. Lafferty

Foreword by Chris Meador
Introduction by Carlos Royal

Copyright © 2013 by Tom Stephan
All rights reserved. No part of this book may be used or reproduced in any manner whatsoever without written permission, except in the case of brief quotations embodied in critical articles or reviews.
Published 2013
Printed by CreateSpace in the United States of America

ISBN-13: 978-1492177302
ISBN-10: 149217730X

Text copyright © 2013 by Tom Stephan
Photographs copyright © 2013 by Tom Stephan, unless otherwise noted.

Cover Photos

Front Cover
The famous barn owl, McGee, heading out to hunt and feed his hungry growing brood.
Photo by Carlos Royal—Used and edited with permission

Back Cover
A successful day of hawking draws to a close. Time to go home.
Photo by author

Dedication

This book is dedicated first and foremost to my mother, Margaret Fisher-Acosta, who at the time of this scribing is 91 years and just as supportive now of my avian efforts as she was in 1960

and to all the "grassroots" raptor conservation organizations I have had the pleasure to know including The California Hawking Club and the American Falconry Conservancy.

The author, hawking a female Finnish Goshawk in subadult plumage.

Table of Contents

Foreword		ix
Preface		xiii
Acknowledgments		xv
From the Author		xvii
Introduction		xxi
Prologue		1
Chapter 1:	From the Beginning	5
Chapter 2:	All About Barn Owls	13
Chapter 3:	Box Design	39
Chapter 4:	Box Construction	59
Chapter 5:	Box Placement	65
Chapter 6:	Box Maintenance	79
Chapter 7:	Attracting Barn Owls	85
Chapter 8:	Electrocution	91
Chapter 9:	Kestrels	101
Chapter 10:	Natural vs. Chemical Rodent Control	107
Chapter 11:	US Law Regarding Migratory Birds of Prey (raptors)	113
Chapter 12:	Orphaned Owlets and Injured Owls	119
Chapter 13:	Domestication of Barn Owls	123
Chapter 14:	Memories and Anecdotes	129
Afterwords		163
Technical Terms/Glossary		165
Index		171
About the Author		177
Photo Credits		183
Contact Information		184

Strix, a fledgling owlet, hides among the leaves
Photo by Colleen Gepp—Used with permission

Foreword

by Chris Meador

When I was about 8 years old, a man, or more specifically, a falconer, came to my elementary school in Ramona, CA. He brought with him a number of falcons and hawks. I remember it to this day, about 20 years later. This man proceeded to tell us schoolchildren that raptors were dinosaurs, that raptors ate practically everything, putting them at the top of the food chain, that raptors were utilized by humans for hunting for thousands of years (and still are today), that raptors lead intricate lives, that a single pair of barn owls could eat 2,000 gophers in a year, and that raptors were in danger of losing critical habitat they needed to survive—my jaw was on the ground. Just seeing these birds eye-to-eye was stunning. That day changed my life. The man with the falcons and hawks was Tom Stephan.

Now I am the Assistant Director of a leading raptor research, education, and conservation organization. I spend my time studying raptors, especially golden eagles, teaching kids and adults alike about the importance or raptors, and trying to save land for wildlife and plants to thrive on. I teach many of the same topics that Tom taught me many years ago.

Tom introduced me to many new experiences. We would go out into the wild land, flying his falcons, looking for wildlife.

There is nothing more powerful than to watch a peregrine falcon (the fastest animal on the planet) hunt. A peregrine falcon circles higher into the sky until you can hardly see it, even with binoculars. Then, out of nowhere, the falcon drops like a rocket. As it plummets towards earth, you think, there is no way it's going to be able to slow down enough to stop before it smashes into the ground. Somehow, at the last moment before impact with the ground, the falcon begins to pull up in a swooping motion. BOOM—it collides with a duck; there's an explosion of feathers. For a moment you wonder what happened, then the falcon appears and circles back to pick up its meal—just another day for a peregrine falcon. This feat is evolutionary in the fact that a peregrine falcon's body has evolved over thousands of years to allow speeds of over 200 miles per hour!

Tom would also take me out to install barn owl boxes. The best part was going back to boxes he had already put up and seeing the barn owl chicks fledge. This was when the owls first left their home in the box, going out into the world and learning to fly. No owl got it right the first try—they often crashed to the ground in a less than graceful fashion, but improving with every try and never giving up.

Nothing is more important to me than ensuring the long-term survival of people, animals, and plants. Why would you not want all these beings to live healthy and happy lives? Our world has been evolving for billions of years; nature has created a natural balance that should be followed. Failing to follow this balance causes unnecessary suffering. Allowing barn owls to do what they do best, prey upon small rodents,

FOREWORD

is natural. Pesticides have shown over and over again to cause health problems for wild animals, pets, and people, including children. This is not natural and benefits nobody.

Tom's book *Beneficial Barn Owls* serves a much bigger purpose than just providing a safe alternative to rodenticides; it illuminates the serious dangers of these chemicals, silent killers that often go unnoticed. Rodenticide manufacturers must be held responsible for improperly marketing these products as safe. Out-of-sight should not mean out-of-mind.

The widespread and commonly accepted use of rodenticides and other chemicals today would remind Rachael Carson, the famous author/activist/biologist, of her struggles to ban chemicals such as DDT. In the 1960s her, controversial book *Silent Spring* blew the whistle on the dangers of DDT and other poisons, spurring a nationwide ban on many of these harmful chemicals. Why are we again allowing the use of chemicals that significantly harm wildlife and endanger our own health? I thought hindsight was twenty-twenty. Rachael Carson would be rolling over in her grave.

The barn owl box at my parents' house where I grew up has barn owls in it every year. When I visit my parents' house in the spring, I hear the chicks calling out to their parents, I see the chicks' mom and dad hunting, and I think to myself, "This is awesome!" Tom and I have dedicated our lives to preserving and protecting wildlife. We hope you will join us in spreading the word that avoiding rodenticide is as easy as putting up a wood box and saying "no" to poison. Nature has the easy answer—barn owls!

Strix, a heart among the leaves
Photo by Colleen Gepp—Used with permission

Preface

My purpose in writing this book is to promote an understanding of and enthusiasm for the use of barn owls as natural rodent control.

My goal is two-fold. I seek a worldwide recognition of barn owls as the premier rodent control method. My hope is that this will lead to a ban on chemical rodenticides. The two are not compatible if one wishes to harbor nesting pairs of owls.

A young owlet, still adorned with fluffy pantaloons nestles among the leaves in a tree adjacent to his home
Photo by Colleen Gepp—Used with permission

Acknowledgments

I wish to thank the following wonderful people:

My wife Paula, who should be sainted,

Rick Windle, the special genius behind
the nest box designs.

Carlos and Donna Royal
and their grandson, Austin Faure,

Bert and Sharon Kersey,

Chris Meador,

Timothy Ann Hunt,

Dr. David Metzgar,

My good friend of all these years, botanist and
biologist, Fred Sproul,

Those who contributed photos;
Katherine Bannister, John David Bittner, Les Blenkhorn, Becky Boberg, Steve Chindgren, Stephen Ford, Bob Franz, Andrew and Colleen Gepp, Charles Gilband, Lauren Greider, Craig Hesse, Joshua Myers, Sara Rosenbaum, Doug Sooley, Robert Weigand,

Peter Schouten, who graciously allowed me the use of
his painting of *Archeopteryx*,

Charlie Khoury,

and

My editor, Dorothy Lafferty, who will put
up with just about anything.

Peeking out at the world around him
Photo by Colleen Gepp—Used with permission

From the Author

In grade school I liked two things, daydreaming and reading books. I took exception to negative connotations my elders attached to daydreaming. To me it was the use of my imagination. I could leave the classroom prison by letting my mind roam at will.

Books often played a role in this imaginative escapism. I enjoyed classic American science fiction by authors such as H.G. Wells and Jules Vern. Books were wonderful worlds conveyed to me at my fingertips. Books inspired a physical escapism, too, encouraging my explorations of the ocean or hills whenever I could get away from class.

I loved adventure stories, as well, like *White Fang* by Jack London and a lesser known but, in my mind's eye, equal book entitled *Desert Dog* by Jim Kjelgaard. Of my favorites is *Wild Animals I Have Known* by Ernest Thompson Seton. This book stood out from all the rest. I kept re-reading it. The library sent me notices. It was difficult to part with it. I wanted to write a book such as that someday.

Because of Seton's influence on me, I took it upon myself at the tender age of eight to get to know the individual wild animals inhabiting the canyon behind my La Jolla Shores childhood home. Birds of all forms and their habits were logged into my notebook, as well as skunks, bobcats, and grey foxes.

By spending time with these creatures, I learned their habits and the densities of the local populations at an early age. Later it would serve me well, as I could easily recognize when an area like the Ramona Grasslands were being impacted. (At the time of writing, June 2013, a large portion of this precious raptor habitat has already been cleared by the County of San Diego for a housing development.)

**McGee, delivering dinner to the eagerly awaiting owlets
(The box owner has made a few modifications to the box)**
Photo by Carlos Royal—Used with permission

From the Author

Older treatises about wildlife invariably speak of species in terms of their worth to man. For example, barn owls were promoted as "beneficial" rodent killers, and goshawks were derided as "chicken hawks." Bounties were paid for the lifeless corpses of many birds of prey not long before I arrived in this world. I recall Rachel Carson's *Silent Spring* drawing this unenlightened era to a dramatic close or at least loudly ending its public celebration.

This rating of a species based on how they immediately benefitted or inconvenienced mankind was repugnant to me even as a child . I knew that these species could not live alone from each other or their habitat. In turn I also knew that we could not ultimately survive without all of them. "Look deeply into nature and you will understand everything better." This quote by Albert Einstein was, to me then, as pure and simple as a Haiku.

Today the labeling of someone as a "Neanderthal" is just as tasteless. These complex and capable hominid ancestors contributed greatly to our present form with their music, art, and religion.

If the reader will bear with me, I wish to label barn owls here in this book as "Beneficial Barn Owls," as their contributions to mankind are often direct and quite obvious. Moreover, they truly are beneficial in more ways than may immediately meet the imagination's eye.

To realize the immediate benefits, one must only watch as the owls' ghostly forms draw out of the dark to a nest box in your back yard, often carrying a pest that has recently been driving you to utter frustration. With greater familiarity, more subtle value becomes apparent as well. What is more, having a close relationship with a wild animal helps us understand the needs of the wildlife upon which we are so often blindly dependent.

Thomas N. Stephan

Molly, the world's most famous barn owl, shortly after moving into the box (two years after it was installed)
Photos by Carlos Royal—Used with permission

Introduction
by Carlos Royal

In thinking back, I find it absolutely amazing that one phone call could change a person's life so dramatically and put in motion events that would touch the lives of over 21 million people around the world, but that is what happened when I called the author of this book, Tom Stephan of Air Superiority. Now, I don't know why I am so surprised. At the bottom of all my emails I have the quote "Decisions determine destiny." I made the decision to make the call and the rest is history, as they say

Let me tell you a short story of what can happen if you put an owl box in your backyard.

Back in 2008 my wife, while relaxing and doing some knitting on a Saturday afternoon, was watching a local TV program about the benefits of having an owl box in your backyard. I was out in my workshop and did not see the show but Donna, my wife, did and she was all excited. After the show she came out to my workshop and told me all about it. She wanted an owl box; she thought it would be really cool to watch owls in our backyard. Our backyard was already like a bird menagerie. We had identified 61 different species of birds that had visited our nature-friendly yard, plus we had watched kestrels, bluebirds, finches, doves, sparrows, hummingbirds, and killdeer all build nests, lay eggs, and raise babies in our backyard, but we had never even seen an owl in the area. I said to Donna, trying to get out of the chore, "But we have never even seen an owl around here." Her reply was, "If you build it, they will come." "Okay," I said with a smile, but like most husbands with other things on their mind, I did nothing about it.

After about two weeks—it might have been three—Donna gave me a little nudge by printing out a set of plans she found on the Internet and placing them right in the middle of my workbench where I could not miss them. Taking the hint, I built an owl box but then there was the issue of how and where to install it. An owl box is not a little birdhouse or at least not the one I had built. It was heavy, big and bulky and it needed to be installed about 15 feet in the air according to the information I could find. I decided instead of risking life and limb, I would ponder the situation for a solution.

Three, maybe four, months of pondering had passed by; I had basically put the owl box out of my mind when Donna asked me, "When is the owl box going to be installed?" Thinking fast, I said I had decided to call the man she had seen on TV because I didn't have what was needed to install the owl box I had built. I then explained I didn't have a 24-foot ladder that would be needed if I were going to install it on the RV garage, and I didn't have a 20-foot pole if I were going to install it on a pole. Let's see . . . could I think of anymore excuses?

Introduction

Donna extended her hand and in it was a piece of paper with Tom's phone number on it. I guess she had come to the same conclusion I had. If she were going to get an owl box installed someone else was going to have to install it.

I called Air Superiority and left my number. In the meantime, I went out to his website and looked at his owl boxes. They did not look like the one I had built. After seeing what he had, I knew what I wanted. I wanted the one with a camera. I had just gotten off the computer when Tom called me back. I didn't even tell him I had built an owl box; I just wanted the one with the camera.

The next day Tom installed an owl box with a camera in our backyard. Wires were strung along the fence and in through the family-room window to our TV. Cool, we could see the inside of the owl box on our big screen TV. I asked Tom how soon before we would get an owl. He said he couldn't say for sure but maybe right away. So we waited and watched, and we waited and watched and we waited and we watched some more. At first we checked the owl box camera almost every day; with nature, one must have lots of patience, but after about a year our patience was running out and at a year and a half, I disconnected the camera from the TV. Remember, when I said we had never seen an owl in our area? Well, we still hadn't.

Then in January of 2010, we had a terrific windstorm where the wind blew so hard it blew our fence down. The next morning, I went out to survey the damage and my neighbor, who was already out surveying the damage, said to me, "Did you hear all the noise and racket last night?" I thought he meant the windstorm, so I said, "You mean the wind storm?" "No," he said, "I mean the owls!" as he pointed to the owl box.

I forgot about the damage and looked for the wires and ran them through the window to the TV and re-hooked them up. Holding my breath, I turned on the TV. Lo and behold, there stood a little owl standing on one leg, looking right at us. At first we thought it was a baby owl as we had never seen a barn owl before. At the time, I don't think I even knew what a barn owl was, but there was something totally captivating about watching this owl with her head tilted with an inquisitive look. "Are you watching me?"

The first night a male owl showed up and we quickly realized she was no baby owl and that she would soon be laying some fertile eggs. As I said, our backyard is basically a bird and nature menagerie. We had gotten into the habit of naming all the birds and animals that came to visit, and this was no exception. Sitting on the couch Donna said, "She looks like a Molly to me," and I said, "If she is Molly then he must be McGee," vaguely remembering the old radio show *Fibber McGhee and Molly* from my childhood.

While many books are written about the effects of bringing nature into your backyard, I would like to join Tom in pointing out the beneficial effects of just watching nature in your backyard. It can be so fun, entertaining, and therapeutic. I believe after you read this book you will want an owl box in your backyard, too.

Introduction

Now, to finish the story, we decided to share what we were watching with my mother and sister who lived about 200 miles away. My mom was 95 at the time. Our grandson, Austin Faure, suggested we live stream The Owl Box on _Ustream.tv_ on the Internet. So we did, not really thinking about anybody else watching. The next thing we knew The Owl Box had gone viral and millions were watching around the world 24 hours a day. We were in local and national newspapers, and we were on local and national television news shows. Books were written, cartoons drawn and a multitude of products sold but, more importantly, we received hundreds of emails from people suffering from a variety of ailments, all saying basically the same thing—watching Molly had taken away their pain.

I can't guarantee if you put an owl box in your backyard you will become famous as we did, but here is what I can guarantee you. You will be helping nature, you will help eradicate rodents from your area without poisons, and you will have a lot of wonderful entertainment

With almost 25,000 owl boxes installed, the world owes a debt of gratitude to Tom Stephan.

Thank you, Tom.

One of the author's clients took this photo of his box and made it into Christmas cards that are sent out every year. Four juvenile barn owlets (left, two females -right, two males)
Photo by Bob Franz—Used with permission

Prologue

From early elementary age we all have been taught about the "terrible lizards" known as dinosaurs. I'm sure we could all recognize the gentle, lumbering Apatosaurus (previously known as Brontosaurus) and the fearsome, predatory Tyrannosaurus rex. This old, incredibly diverse, family tree of dinosaurs ruled the earth for hundreds of millions of years. Split into two groups, or trunks, of the family tree, the entire superorder was wiped out by a catastrophic asteroid impact at Chixulub in Mexico and its aftermath. But one tiny stem—a petiole—survived.

One type of dinosaur (or at least its descendants) lives today. All birds are a type of beaked dinosaur with feathers. These "birds" are members of bipedal (two legged), carnivorous, theropod dinosaurs called "Coelurosaurs" (see loora soars). All birds are very closely related to some very famous names in the Coelurosauria group, such as Tyrannosaurs, Velociraptors and Oviraptors, to name but an interesting few.

There is an ancestor to all modern owls in the Strigiformes line that is found as fossilized specimens dating back some seventy million years ago The rest of the dinosaurs were gone by 64 million years BP (before present). What this means is, at the very least, the ancestors of our common barn owls lived and flew alongside these great beasts.

As Professor Paul wrote in his excellent book *Dinosaurs of the Air,* "Barn owls hunted the ancestors of our ancestors from between the legs of dinosaurs."[1] These ancestors were tiny shrew like mammals, or basal eutherians.

Then the end came for Dinosauria. At the time the dinosaurs were becoming extinct, there were three orders of "dino/birds." Two were birds in every way but had rows of wickedly sharp teeth set in powerful jaws. The great beasts and most late Cretaceous birds went extinct. A prerequisite for survival would have been the ability to feed on small prey, be nocturnal and live in burrows, much like the burrowing owls we know today. This mass extinction left only the birds with beaks or "Neornithes."

I often wonder why the birds survived and all the rest went extinct. If we can find the answer to that question, it is probable that we will have a good handle on why the rest disappeared.

After the extinction, a great vacuum was present. It was soon filled by gigantic mammals and tiny dinosaurs—the birds. Turnabout is allowed with Mother Nature. Although small now, these birds radiated into every niche one may care to

---

[1] Gregory S. Paul; *Dinosaurs of the Air: The Evolution and Loss of Flight in Dinosaurs and Birds* (Baltimore, Maryland: The Johns Hopkins University Press, April 1, 2002) ISBN-10: 0801867630—ISBN-13: 978-0801867637

PROLOGUE

imagine. Some lost flight altogether. Birds that once flew but no longer do are called "neoflightless." Some dino/birds were neoflightless as well, as were velociraptors. These powerful turkey sized maniraptors folded their wings in the same manner as flying birds, so they, at one time, flew, just as did modern ostriches.

This rapid evolution of birds occurred about fifty million years ago in the Cenozoic Era. Some were massive flyers with wingspans of 16 feet or more. Some speedy members of the parrot family became modern falcons. Parrots are tropical for the most part. Falcons and their ancestors, the peregrines, now live in all habitats. Greenland, one of the coldest climes on the planet is the world's bastion of breeding falcons.

Owls, as I said, were already present, but now there were many new forms including the massive eagle owls. North America has only one eagle owl, the great horned owl. As "great" as it is, it has no horns, but tufted feathers atop its great skull. Many other species of owls have these tufts leading to some confusion. If I were president of the Audubon Society, I would change the name from great horned owl to American eagle owl. Because—well, that's what it is.

Barn owls are quite the survivors, having witnessed "the great passing" of all their kin save a few. Barn owls are very active compared to most owls, a term called tachymetobolic. They go go go, motor scooter style, burning calories. They also take in calories. Oh, brother! Do they take in calories!

In the quintessential book *Life Histories of North American Birds of Prey* by Arthur Cleveland Bent, there is an account of an early 1900s farmer named W.L. Finley. Mr. Finley came into possession of a young barn owl who had recently learned to stand upright. This owlet was given eight dead mice that it swallowed whole in rapid succession. "The ninth followed all but the tail which for some time hung out of the bird's mouth."[2]

Within an hour this raptor consumed four additional mice! This caused Mr. Finley to surmise that if a single owl was only satiated after consuming over a dozen mice, what impact would an entire brood of young owls and their two parents have on the vermin of a community?

After twenty years of nest box building and installation I think I have found the answer.

---

[2]Arthur Cleveland Bent, *Life Histories of North American Birds of Prey* (Mineola, NY: Dover Publications, February, 1968) ISBN-10: 0486209318 — ISBN-13: 978-0486209319

Chapter 1

From the Beginning

The California canyons of La Jolla Shores in the 1950s were, for an active, nature loving boy like me, a Shangri La of sage, toyon and lemon berry bushes. I was fascinated by pepsis wasps, tarantulas, alligator lizards, king snakes, rattlesnakes and road runners. My mother was very supportive of my hiking and note taking. So was a special man, named Sam Hinton, who worked at Scripps Institution of Oceanography.

One of my favorite ways to experience nature was to climb under that vegetation and wait quietly. After some time, the wildlife would begin to come out into view and go about their way. Many hours these creatures filled my young eyes and mind in amazed contemplation.

For me, as a child, birds were the most fascinating of the "community" of animals found among the vegetation now called Coastal Sage Scrub. They would do the "Towhee Two Step," sing, fight, play and socialize. Then in an instant, they'd simply fly away. I was amazed.

I was then attending a Catholic academy. My second-grade teacher informed the class that we had a new assignment. We were each to produce a report in one week about a wild animal—any wild animal.

A week later it began.

Come report time, we were all asked, one by one, to stand next to our respective desks and tell the class what species we were to report on. To the teacher's and the class' amusement and at my expense, I naively said, "Dinosaurs."

When the chuckling died down my educator calmly informed me, "No, Tom, it has to be a living animal that you must report on."

I was red faced with embarrassment. I quickly countered with "I'll do it on golden eagles!"

"OK, good, Tom. Why golden eagles?"

"Because they remind me of dinosaurs."

They were really laughing now. I wanted to dig a hole and hide.

I often wish I had a time machine, because I'd be the one laughing. I was right all along. Even in second grade, I had nailed it, but I didn't find that out for a decade. That was when I read in biology class about an animal named "Archeopteryx," meaning "ancient wing."

The Archeopteryx, a "dino/bird," was pulled from a slate quarry in Germany in 1860 and was initially described in 1861 by Christian Erich Hermann von Meyer. Here was T-Rex in miniature—cast in stone. It had teeth and claws but was covered in feathers. Not just a simple matting of down, but flight or "curvaceous" feathers. The presence of curvaceous feathers is where the flight rubber hits the road.

Was it a bird or a dinosaur? The best minds of the day could not agree. The question was begged, "What determines a bird?"

"If it has feathers is that a bird? But it had teeth."

Archaeopteryx
Illustration by Peter Schouten of Studio Schouten (www.studioschouten.com). From *Feathered Dinosaurs—the Origin of Birds*. Used with permission.

"If it flew, was it then that it became a bird?"

The debate raged.

The kicker was that a quiet genius had just produced a book entitled *The Origin of Species* a scant two years before in 1859. The book and the fossil stood the scientific community and the world on its ear. "I'll be a monkey's uncle," was the gaff. I figure why not. Good as any.

There were many dino/Birds. Dyonychus was a favorite. It still is. I began to read about the people who dug them up and wrote the papers about them, putting their reputations on the block. I liked the worker John Ostrum. His papers about this animal raised from the Morrison formation of North America detailed that it is more of a giant flightless bird than a slow squat reptile.

Here was bird in transition to becoming a dinosaur. Or was it the other way around? In any event, it stood about as high as a man (or a woman) and was a very capable predator, equipped with all the talons, teeth, and muscles to subdue strong quarry. Oh, yes, and it had feathers. Like a huge "velociraptor" of Mongolia's "Flaming Cliffs," it was the stuff of a boy's nightmare fascinations.

Paleontologist Ostrum re-proposed an idea that was first raised by Thomas Huxley, aka "Darwin's Bulldog," in the mid 1800s that dinosaurs were more like giant, flightless birds than lizards. The oldest known dinosaur was possibly "Eoraptor, or "dawn thief" as it was the first known upright bipedal dinosaur, dating back some 229 million years BP.

I was searching about for pictures of golden eagles to enter into my report when I was handed a *National Geographic* magazine article entitled "A day in the Life of an Indian Prince," by soon-to-become biologist and falconers, Frank and Jean Craighead.

The Craigheads told of the monarch practicing falconry, the oldest known field sport. He was depicted trapping, taming, training, and hunting with formerly wild birds of prey—what we refer to as "raptors" today.

I was a boy transfixed. I knew what it was to have a goal. I wanted to be falconer. As a falconer I would have a cool pet and I would be able to continue running around the canyons and fields. Grownups were telling me, "You'll have to give that up when you become older." I decided the heck with that.

The author training a female Finnish Goshawk.
Photo by Joshua Myers—Used with permission

I pored over the article. I rented books on falconry from the library. My mother was so proud as this was some kind of milestone. I drew sketches of falconers hunting with their charges. Known as the "Sport of Kings," it was all the rage for the crowned heads of Europe from Marco Polo to the invention of the shotgun.

My father added that there was a Prussian Duke on his family's side. It turned out it was a Bavarian Count, Heinrich Stephan of

Eberstein Castle. He asked me if a Duke was not good enough for me? My intuition tells me this man was a falconer as well. It just has to be in my DNA.

Soon I was into it with both feet and trying my best to catch one of these elusive birds. In the process I became quite adept at the climbing of trees. "Flying dinosaurs" nested there it seemed. Later in life, I took the avocation of tree surgeon as a way to keep myself from those office "cages" my parents had prescribed for me earlier in life.

Alt-Eberstein Castle near Baden-Baden, Germany, the ancestral home of the author's family
Photo © Baden-Baden Kur & Tourismus—Used with permission

Fast forward 20 years. I was jotting down a tree trimming proposal for a nice lady in a posh neighborhood called Pauma Valley. There it was—an empty barn owl nesting box on a low tree limb of an ancient California Sycamore tree.

I mentioned that she was not likely to get owls in the box as it

The author installing a box in a tree in Ramona, California

was too low and too close to the kitchen window. An added hindrance was that the box had a doorway on the end that afforded no privacy to the owls, privacy that would allow them to nest comfortably.

Then the light went on. If she would sign up, for no extra charge, I would move the box up high where it indeed would get owls. This deal sweetener was just the ticket. I moved the box on Wednesday and she had a pair of barn owls on Saturday. Bingo! Her friend wanted them as well.

A friend of hers who was over playing a hand or two of Bridge that day, noticed the birds in the box. It became the topic of the morning as everyone gathered around the window. It seems that the owls were just as inquisitive about the humans as the humans were about them. Everyone was staring at each other from inside his/her respective house.

My client informed me during a telephone conversation later that day that her late husband had put the box up standing on a ladder some years before. He was sad that he never got any residents for his wife and had since passed away. The resident owls filled a void in her life.

It felt good making people feel good. Nearly twenty-five thousand boxes later (and counting) it still does.

"The owls were just as inquisitive about the Humans as the humans were about them."
Photo by Colleen Gepp—Used with permission.

Chapter 2

All About Barn Owls

Barn Owl Biology

Barn owls are members of the order *Strigiformes*. They are one of the older or "basal" forms of owls. Fossil scratchers like to use the term basal as it does not sound as derogatory as the word "primitive" does.

If barn owls are primitive, then this is a feather in their cap as they then have lived through tough times and persisted. They are still here after much change because they have a body plan that works. Birds in general are a marvel.

Birds can run around on the ground, fly out to sea, swim or fly underwater to catch fish, and fly home. The only other vertebrate that can fly are bats. Bats hate to walk so much they hang upside down.

One bird, the Wandering Albatross, spends almost all of its life in flight, landing only to breed and feed. It is difficult to measure the distances an albatross travels each year, but there is documentation of one banded albatross travelling 6000 km (3728 miles) in 12 days.

Some birds can fly so well they migrate over the highest mountains in the world, at 30,000 feet at night, in winter and know where they are going and arrive without freezing to death. Some mammals migrate, but do so very slowly and with difficulty out of necessity to find new sources of food and water. Birds, however, migrate great distances with, what seems to humans, apparent ease.

Barn owls here in California do not migrate, *per se*. When the young leave the protection of their parents they just wander off to the four points of the compass. Florida as well. In the northeastern United States the young appear to move southward somewhat to warmer weather. The survivors return then the following spring. The adults do not appear to leave their hard won nesting sites.

The plumage of barn owls "(Tyto alba) varies from light to dark morphs. All of the barn owls that I have seen save one in the Galápagos Islands were white on the belly and crop for the male and a creamy buff on the belly for females. The top of the wings and back of this species is an odd sort of orange-gold with little flecks and spots of lavender and barring.

The feathers of birds come in three types. Type one is a stem with a single strand of down. This is their initial down they are born with. Type two feathers are the same quill with many strands of down. Type 3 feathers that conform to the shape of the bird or aid in its flight and maneuvering. These are the curvaceous feathers.

Then there are lateral branches and twigs. These are called rachis and barbs. The barbs are the world's first "Velcro" and zip together making a seal for the wing's sail effect. Owls go farther still and have barbulets, which are yet another lateral on the barbs.

To falconers avian plumage is rated from "hard" to "soft." Ravens, peregrine falcons, and waterfowl have some of the hardest plumage. One can hear a raven flying overhead when it beats its wings with a whoosh whoosh.

Owls have the barbulets to soften almost 100% of all noise. Owls give up speed for stealth and it suits them fine. But an owl flushed from its roost in the daytime is a very vulnerable animal indeed because of all the much faster diurnal birds zipping about.

Standing erect, barn owls are quite unique with very little of a tail. This is pronounced by very long tarsi. They seem to be all face and head until they spread their wings and sail off. The wingspread is about a yard and can appear quite large. As a result, I often hear some wild claims about how big they are and how much they weigh.

"It stood this high" some old gent would exclaim, holding his hand up about his waist. I knew he was advanced in age, but I was not aware that he was alive to witness the extinction of the gigantic barn owl "Tyto gigantea" millions of years ago.

Just the sight comparison of birds to mammals is so one-sided. Try and compare a flamingo or bird o' paradise with a bull elephant seal. I can almost smell the seal from here.

Birds' plumage has a wonderful aroma, a bouquet if you will. To bury one's nose in the plumage of a falcon is to breathe in this wonderful bloom. In a way, it is like freshly dried linen when you open the dryer or roasted cashews, only different.

Starting from the owl's feet, the talons are very pointed. They penetrate the hide of rodents and humans alike with ease. They have a zygodactyl or peripheral grip like a parrot or woodpecker with two talons facing forward and two back. This arrangement keeps the prey from sliding out of their grasp laterally.

Among raptors, few birds have this configuration. Most have the more common digit arrangement known as tridactyl – three in front and one in back. This is the foot pattern of the speedier birds. The other (as with a woodpecker, for example) is adapted for clutching the vertical walls of tree trunks. The exception to this rule is the roadrunner whose closest relatives are cavity nesting cuckoos, go figure.

The tendons that are attached to the calf and thigh muscles are strung through sheaths with internal one-way corrugation. When clamped down on prey or my hand for that matter, raptors have to concentrate to let go. It is the exact opposite for them for grasping. That is almost involuntary.

Birds' bones, like their feathers are hollow for lightness. Both of these features were present before this group of birds achieved flight. One well known paleontologist states that there have been six other flying theropods before these modern day birds with beaks. What captivating birds have flown through the forests' canopies of long ago? There were tiny hunters with flight feathers on their feet. There were also carnivorous birds with the body plan of a Capuchin monkey, designed to run speedily and fly through the densest of foliage.

The legs prop up an erect bipedal animal with hot blood and an appetite to match. Fully loaded in the down stroke of flying, the breast musculature pull down strings and struts above the shoulders like a bow. Fully loaded in the down position, the bow snaps the wings back upward to ready the wings for

Lucy, a Peregrine/Barbary falcon hybrid, bred by Les Boyd
Photo provided by the author—taken by an unidentified attendee at Hawk Watch

the next flap down. The wings flip up and forward with a thrusting motion. This is achieved with a specialized wrist bone or "semilunate carpal" that is shaped like a banana. This adaptation allows the primary flight feathers to snap forward to bite into new air, pushing it down and back to propel our bird to a rodent, a branch, a nest, or a new continent.

Birds have the fastest reaction time in earth's nature. The lower mandible of a skimmer can snap shut in a fraction of a second. Once at sunset, I witnessed a hundred mourning

Clarise, a Aplamado/Peregrine hybrid—the only such hybrid known in the world at the time. Bred by Richard Jones.
Photo provided by the author—taken by an unidentified attendee at Hawk Watch

doves settling in a 75-foot long row of tall, very dense maraporum bushes for the night's roost. The foliage was so thick, one could not see through more than about two feet of it. A zipping sharp-shinned hawk entered one end of the row suddenly at about 80 MPH, then exited the other end in about a second and a half. The escaping doves were piling out for their lives like the pattern of an electromagnetic field. The hawk could have caught a dinner—or not. I will never know as it was gone that quick. How does a Harris's Hawk dive headlong into cactus after a rabbit and emerge without spines? I cannot tell you how, only that I have seen it happen.

Next is the chart house of our bird, the head. This marvelous critter, the barn owl, is equipped with superman vision and echo locating radar. Their ears are so acute they can hear the heartbeat of someone standing under the nest box. They can hear rodents such as pocket gophers excavating soil from their burrows with much acuity. They have time to approach, hover over the hole and when the gopher pushes dirt out— plunk—crunch— and off the owl goes, back to the nest, to drop off another rodent. They make short work of a seemingly impossible job. It's little wonder that barn owls have persisted for nearly a hundred million years.

The beak can nurture tiny helpless chicks, or tear apart the rat that was, just a moment ago, chewing into your garage.

One of the more memorable occurrences in watching Molly and her young happened during the second clutch. Carrie, the youngest of the surviving owlets in that clutch, had developed some kind of eye infection. She could not open her eyes at all because they were so matted shut. Among the online chatters there was much speculation and worry that she was blind and would never survive. Some quoted so-called "experts" and said there was absolutely no hope.

The chatters watched Molly draw Carrie under her wing and very gently use her beak to peck all the crusted matter out of Carrie's eyes. She did this repeatedly over the course of two or three days. Of course, within a couple of days, Carrie was fully recovered and doing fine. It was amazing to see Molly's gentleness with that beak that just moments before had been shredding a rodent.

A barn owlet that just learned to stand can shovel down a

gopher or rat whole without the benefit of hands. One can see the little bird's mouth stretching to new apertures with a glance. Down into a highly acidic gastrointestinal tract goes the mammal, soon to become what I like to refer to as "liquid rats." The waste product is both numbers 1 and 2 (urine and feces) in a single push. Now that's efficiency.

Courtship

Here in southern California barn owl courtship begins as soon as the rainy season does. That is usually about the new year, later if the rains are late. This behavior would be later in the season the farther north one may travel. The male will locate several nest boxes and or sites if he has them and begin his calling in them one by one. In the very first nesting box that I installed on a steel post and pole method, a box in the front yard, the calling began about Christmas time.

This calling, repeated clicks ending in a plaintive screech, went on almost all night for about a week. One night a female landed in a nearby Sycamore tree and screeched back as if to say "Yeah, waddya want?" The male screeched a couple of times very excitedly then exited the box. He flew upward in spiraling circles around the tree clicking the entire time up to and higher than her perch at about 50' up. I realized then that I was witnessing a courting flight barn owl style.

When he was almost out of view above the tree, he dove or "stooped" past the female owl missing her by an inch and with as much aplomb as he could muster, pulled out of the dive and shot immediately into the box at almost full speed. He knew that her eyes would be upon this brash ego maniac due to the near miss and would notice him enter the box and beckon, "Come hither."

He began to call incessantly and quite loudly. So much so in fact that the box was shaking from his calls. He really gave the appearance of giving it everything he had. She was there in the tree for a minute or so, then flew off. Barn owls are much like humans, I gathered.

He kept up the calling unabated that night and the next. The third night I was alerted to the box being inhabited by both owls as there was quite a disturbance coming from within. I walked closer. Evidently the female had just entered the nest box. She was finally excited by the persistent calling of the male each night within her foraging habitat. The clicking and screeching was a raucous corraboree with constant calling and wobbling of the nesting box. This is what Carlos Royal's neighbor must have

A male waits for his mate to approve his choice of boxes
Photo by Colleen Gepp—Used with permission

witnessed the night Molly went into McGee's lair.

At first I wished I had put a camera in there, then I thought better of it. I would not want anyone filming my wife and me on our wedding night! Later I thought better of that yet again. I would have had the only footage of the courtship behavior of pairing barn owls. It would have been great stuff for aspiring biologists.

Egg Laying and Hatching

The eggs are laid soon thereafter in series and not all at once like ducks, chickens or sea turtles. The eggs are roundish and small and give this author the impression more of ping pong balls than of chicken's eggs.

This batch of eggs or "clutch" is initially laid on the bare wood of the nesting box. There is no need to exacerbate the amount of material that will eventually build up inside the box with wood shavings or other human imported nesting material.

Once I installed a nest box for a gentleman who lived in the desert north of Los Angeles. This area of Antelope Valley is very windy. The box fluttered on the pole three to four nights a week. The owls laid their eggs on the bare wood. The parents evidently being so busy with their nuptials that neither thought of making a proper nest. He had three owlets his first year. I asked him, "How do they hatch scrambled eggs?" Another marvel of adaptation.

The female at my house began scratching the bare wood as if

there was a thick layer of sand or oak duff that would naturally be present at the site. Next year she had plenty of material to make a bowl-shaped depression in which to lay her eggs. This is called the "scrape" and is simply a divot.

The eggs usually number about 7-12 in a clutch. This is a gargantuan amount compared to other native raptors—yet another indication that, unlike all the modern birds that surround them, barn owls come from a time long forgotten.

Molly and the six eggs of her fist clutch
During the heat of the day the brooding female will often stand aside the eggs, often exhibiting this behavior to achieve egg weight loss if the eggs are too "wet." If they are lacking in hydration or "crispy" she will stay down on them.
Photo by Donna Royal—Used with permission

In a little less than a month, the eggs will begin to hatch. The chick inside the egg will begin to peck at the crown of the egg with a bump on the upper mandible especially designed for this purpose called "the egg tooth."

Once a hole is poked through the shell the chick has "pipped" and will begin to squeak. This is thought by some to be the origin of the word "pipsqueak." Mother begins talking in soft tones of encouragement all the while and baby calls back. This bond is great fun to watch whether it be watching barn owls on your TV or peregrine falcons on a monitor.

The chick stays in the egg breathing air for the first time as the membrane of blood vessels surrounding the chick desiccate. Once the blood in the membrane has gone from outside to the inside of the chick, the chick begins the arduous task of hatching. The chick works diligently hammering away at the top of the shell with a specialized muscle on the back of its neck. Where does the chick get a muscle, having never made any exercise before? Another wonderment.

Once the lid is off the chick will struggle out of the shell and give the appearance of a baby dinosaur. The chick does not eat for another 24 hours or so as it must first use up the attached yolk sack. This is an effective lunch box for its journey to the out-of-doors.

Here begins what I call the 10% factor. About 10% of the eggs are infertile or "addled" and will never hatch. On average, another 10% of the hatchlings will not survive. In turn, 10% of the chicks will not fledge and so forth and so on, with an ultimate juvenile survival rate of about 1-3 out of ten chicks earning a degree to qualify as a breeding adult.

Rearing the Young

Within 24 hours the chicks are ready for their first meal. The mother's frighteningly powerful beak is now used to gently and most tenderly present tiny morsels of a rodent to the young. A bit is pulled from the animal and the meat held between the mandibles as the parent whispers a low screech. The chick reacts by lifting its head up as best as it can and opening its beak in anticipation of the morsel. Very little is eaten the first meal. That changes rapidly and in a big way.

Within days the chicks eat great quantities of food and are quite ravenous. Within a few weeks the young are standing upright and most prey items are swallowed whole. Gophers, rats and mice are down the hatch in short order.

Food presented to the young are grabbed and eaten as an 1900 falconry book described as being "no better behaved than an American traveller [*sic*] at a roadside feeding-place, or a dowager at a ball-supper.[1]"

Half grown raptors consume huge amounts of protein. Gyrfalcon chicks eat an astounding amount of very expensive, high protein quail. Over 70% of all protein consumed by falcons, hawks and barn owlets goes to feather growth. Taking into account that the owlet must grow bones, organs and muscle mass and weigh as much as its parents in a few short months, this is quite a lot of food indeed.

Raptors have the fastest growth curves of any vertebrate. Their close, but unfortunately extinct cousins, the Tyrannosaurs, like Tyrannosaurs rex, grew from a chicken-sized hatchling to a seven ton monster in five seasons. Some of the minds tasked with these studies conclude that this

---

[1] E.B. Mitchell; *The Art and Practice of Hawking* (London: Methuen & Co., 1900) p. 62.

species had to be pack animals to supply mountains of meat to their young. A pack of Tyrannosaurs. Oy vey!

At this stage there is no small amount of competition for those prey items. Some chicks are too puny to compete and give up the ghost here. Once dead they get trampled into the "cookie" if small, or taken away by the parents if odoriferous. It's the same with uneaten parts of large prey items like cottontail rabbits. Where they take them I do not know. No one seems to know. Far away I do know.

The young have replaced their first set of down by now and have a second set when they start to stand. This in turn is molted again for their juvenile plumage proper (curvaceous feathers and more down). After that set is in they will begin to flap inside the box to build up muscle. This is referred to as "paddling" or "rowing."

Paddling for all she's worth
Photo by Carlos Royal—Used with permission

Copious quantities of molted down are

billowing out of the box when this rowing occurs. Often two or more young will row at the same time. This reminds me of the old World War II films of aircraft carrier fighter planes warming up their engines. It appears to the uninitiated that there is not enough room in the box due to the youngs' wings brushing against the walls of the box. This is not the case and they take confines in stride. Barn owls can nest and rear a clutch of owlets in very small spaces.

Once I saw a barn owl mother that had chosen a desert barn for her home. She had found a cavity at the top, behind the sheet rock siding within the barn. With the metal skin exposed to the full fury of a Borrego Springs summer sun and the sheet rock siding, she had wedged herself on a 2"x4". They raised three young there that fledged and flew away. Amazing.

I once had a test kestrel nesting box on a power pole (much to the power company's chagrin). The first year I observed that I had made the round doorway hole a little too small. So I put on my hooks and climbed up. Using my chainsaw, I opened up the hole—way open—so not to have to make the trip again. Come the following rains I had a pair of barn owls nest in the diminutive nest box. There was nothing I could do ethically or within the law. So I just let it be a natural history lesson. She raised two chicks with not one juvenile mortality.

It is at this time of paddling that the large owlets begin to lose their fear of the doorway and are more curious about what is out there. They soon discover that being in the doorway means being first fed. The jostling of the weaker owls to the rear and stronger to the doorway now occurs.

"So? What's it like out there?"
Photo by Carlos Royal—Used with permission

Owlets fall out prematurely on occasion. This happens in natural nest sites as well as in nest boxes.

Advances in nest box design is part of my job description. Shelves or "porches" are showing promise in allowing safer fledging. The science of making large bird houses borders on the science of airplane construction. These nest boxes with porches must not have adverse effects due to the interaction of design and wind especially when mounted on poles . Wobbling is a constant problem with new designs that must be overcome.

Chicks and fledglings will also abandon the box in heat waves. One spring it was 103° on April 3rd in San Diego County. Clients were calling constantly. It was very sad. This was yet another lesson in my learning curve with regards to box placement. The best place to attract a pair of barn owls was no longer the best place to install the box. Shade is always now on my mind inland from the coast.

Juvenile mortality is never higher than when then owlets are wandering about on the ground. Clients informed of this are adamant they do not have raccoons in their suburban home neighborhood. All it takes is to have a nest full of screeching and begging young owlets to attract predators of any species.

Coyotes are especially fond of barn owls—young or old. Great horned owls and crows are the chief killers. Here in San Diego crows are the greatest force to be contended with. If an owl is found in the daytime the finding crow will sound a staccato alarm call until the surrounding trees are covered with a hundred or more cawing, complaining crows. When their numbers

A Murder of Crows
©Can Stock Photo Inc./mbudley—Used under license

reach saturation, they will begin the attack. Swooping and pecking at the owl they will flush it repeatedly out into the open where they can attack it better. Soon the barn owl succumbs to the stress of the onslaught and is killed.

This is the gauntlet all barn owls run in order to become "wise old owls." If they live through this first encounter, they will in all likelihood live many years. "Why do crows hate owls so much?" one may ask. Crows hate all avian predators but love to hate owls. It seems that the bitter taste of crows is not rebuffed by owls. The North American Eagle Owl or "Great Horned Owl" eats crows with regularity as well as skunks. I have no experience with any other animal that can eat its way past this chemical warfare.

When I was young, crows were a woodland creature and feared man. Then about 1970 in Alta Dena, CA there was a change. It seems there are some live oak-filled canyons that were level to some mature landscaping in the backyards of former silent movie stars and the like.

One year a surplus of nesting crows left the crowded colony called a rookery and began to nest in the large trees present in these back yards. This was the moment to eradicate them. A moment lost now, however, as this

The mobster crow
©Can Stock Photo Inc./iperl—Used under license

population has now spread south to Tijuana, Mexico and North to Redding, CA. Millions of city dwelling crows are now a plague and no open hunting season yet as been declared.

These mobsters have little in the way of control nor is any idea to eradicate them good enough for the government agency in charge of migratory birds. They are a health hazard. They dole out millions of hard earned dollars in property and crop damage. They eat endangered song bird eggs. Still they are guarded. All of my clients are forever asking what they can do about them. They are incredulous when I tell them "nothing."

Fledging

The owlets have now advanced to the fledgling stage and are making their first tentative hops out of the nest. This was a huge moment in the Molly box phenomena. Thousands of viewers and chatters held their cyber breaths as the first youngster hopped out on to the provided perch. I too held mine as I was responsible for any mishaps. All went well, however, and this first adventuresome bird soon returned to the safety of the inside of the box. You could see how this affected the other young. Despite their natural-born timidity (a life-saving trait in many instances) they all wanted to do what their older sibling had achieved.

Within days all of the young are out of the nest and clambering around on the branches or terrain. They will flutter down to the ground and run/fly back up the tree trunk to regain the safety of the nest. This is quite a trick and is wholly avian in its madness. Their reptilian roots show for all to interpret during the performance of this behavior.

Within a few weeks the young fly out of the nest to the nearest tree or power pole, etc. and set up "station." The crown of a tree will be adorned with a brood of young barn owls like a gigantic Christmas tree with feathered ornaments. They call all night and can be quite noisy at this time. Care is taken not to place the box close to the client's bedroom window. Some folks like the sound. I do. But I am more bird than human, my wife informs me.

At no other time of the year are the owls killing more rodents than at this midsummer event. Its quite a show. At Craig Hesse's house there is a donated box that has young fledge every year. He invites me down to watch the show unfold every year. The first year he had illuminated the entire area of the box with large lights.

Being an "expert" I would never have thought of doing this, being afraid of disturbing them and all. This was not the case, however, and the young took no notice of the lights or us, for that matter. You may do it to. Just put them up a couple of weeks prior to the fledging so the owls can get used to them. Invite friends and family. Take photos. Please do not touch or disturb the owls, however.

The parents would arrive with a prey item and with much screeching and vying, a food transfer was performed. The parents are only at the tree for a few moments then off to pull deftly yet another gopher or a hapless rat from its haunts. All night this went on. I lost count of the prey items. This fledging is timed for the crescendo of breeding rodents due to the reproduction of any particular spring season.

Back to the box
Photo by Carlos Royal—Used with permission

By dawn the young were sleepy and back for a day's snore. Within days the young were following their parents about and taking the rodent still wiggling on the ground before the parent had a chance to ferry it to them. The fledgling was just a moment away from making its first kill here and soon no longer needed its parent and began to wander off. Soon they were gone to join the thousands of other barn owls who own the night.

The Molt

The molt is a process whereby a bird drops its old plumage as new feathers unfurl in each old feather's place. A curvaceous feather is a marvel of adaptation. Particular genes spur the growth of the feather from out of the follicle or "integument" to unfold into a plume with a pen or "calamus." One of these genes is called "sonic hedgehog." I am not making this stuff up.

One hopes that this process is complete until the entire body is covered in new feathers seasonally. That season typically starts with the bounty of springtime prey species. This is the barn owl's "happy time." Any given stress during the molting process can stop a molt. Once stopped it may not restart.

When this happens in captive female raptors, some falconers will give them beef thyroid gland. Almost invariably, this will "jump start" the process and the molt will start again. These glands contain the hormone "progesterone" and is a quite powerful regimen to administer. This regimen has no effect on the males. I assume some other part of a bull would work for male raptors but as yet I have heard of no one trying this.

Care must be given when medicating the females with this material. I was sent capsule containing about 5 grams of freeze dried thyroid gland from another breeder. No instructions were given and I had a female Harris' s Hawk that had stopped its summer molt in July.

Playing safe I thought, I would give her half a dose/capsule and see how that would effect her. An hour later I came out and observed that she was literally bouncing off of the walls in her mews. She settled down after a while.

After phoning my friend I was embarrassed to find that I had given her many doses and that the capsule contained a summer's worth of dosages. Her molt began the next day with six flight feathers dropped, two per wing and two from her tail. The molt is much more gradual normally, with one wing feather per wing and two tail feathers at a time.

I was once shown a photo of a female goshawk that had been overdosed by mistake and was completely nude of feathers. She had to be kept warm with the aid of a heat lamp for two weeks until she grew a set of down.

The thickness of down is called "loft." Arctic species like snowy owls and gyrfalcons have up to four inches of loft. A great amount of protein is consumed to produce this downy set in short order.

I brooded a young white gyrfalcon female in my living room once. It was so hot for her here in San Diego on a 80° day, that I had to trim off most of the down and put ice packs all around and under her. Even after I added a fan she still gaped. It can be forty degrees below zero in Alaska in springtime where these raptors are indigenous. Normally, as with barn owls, the chicks must be laid upon by their mother to keep them warm.

Birds' molts typically start with the wing feathers closest to the body (called the "secondary" feathers) and two from the tail, then two by two, one per wing, as the spring and summer progresses until the last end wing feathers are molted. These are the primaries—the flight feathers. All the while, the down and other feathers are being replaced. Barn owls wait a bit longer and start their molts about July when the rearing of so many fledglings is almost complete.

The growing feathers need constant grooming called "preening" to ensure the removal of old feathers, dirt and dried blood that could be matted in the birds' plumage. The risk of feather deformation could occur without daily attention to sanitation for their very important plumage. Birds spend many hours a day (or night as the case may be) ensconced in this duty. Molting has the appearance of being an "itchy" time of year.

Birds will preen to remove the unwanted material from the plumage. Then it will dress the plumage paying particular detail to the tail and wing feathers. The uropygial gland lies atop the base of the tail called the "pygostyle." When rubbed, this gland produces a very fine oil. The bird will rub one side of the beak on the gland tip which I call the "zerc fitting." This coats the lower edge of the upper mandible and upper edge of the lower mandible.

Then the flight feathers are seized firmly, one at a time about the base, stripped of dirt and coated with oil all in one pull. The uncoated side of the beak strips away the dirt and the coated trailing edge of the beak leaving a fine layer of dressing. Raptors take great delight in the performance of this operation. I take great delight in watching them take that delight.

When the molt is complete, the bird is equipped with a new set of plumage to last it through the time of year when survival is most pressing—winter. Juvenile raptors strike out on their own during mid-summer. As the fall approaches and temperatures plummet the birds must consume more food to keep warm. There is less food each day until spring comes as this is the only time that prey populations regenerate.

In addition, the days are getting shorter for the diurnal raptors. So there is less time per day to find more food. The parameters are drawing closer. Most birds have the added stress of migration at this time. During winter, mortality cuts through the juvenile bird populations like a scythe.

To survive they will need more than a fine coat of feathers. They must have a superior body, favorable weather, water and food. They must have cover when they need it and luck. Just as luck in combat is to soldiers, wildlife must be lucky to survive, especially their first winter.

Barn owls are survivors and survive they do. They've lived and thrived for thousands of years and are uniquely equipped to continue thriving for many millennia to come. They not only provide the service of rodent control, but entertain us with their antics when they're young, inspire us with their strength and abilities and awe us with their beauty. The world would be a lesser place without these creatures in our midst.

Two barn owlets, surveying their world.
Photo by Craig Hesse—Used with permission.

Chapter 3

Box Design
The evolution of owl nest box designs

Way back in the Civil War, General Robert E. Lee was said to have said, and I paraphrase, "It's not enough to tell your men what to do. One needs to tell them what not to do, as well." With these words from the wise so graciously handed down, I will explain the evolutionary events that led up to my current box designs. In this way, it is my hope that future nest box builders will not make the same mistakes that I have made. Mistakes waste time, making the humans wait, sometimes for years, for owls to inhabit their box. Also bad designs and placement sometimes put undue stress on owls and their young.

When I put my first nest box up for the nice well-heeled lady in Pauma Valley, her friends wanted them as well. I had no plans. My client told me of plans available at the San Diego County office. I procured a set of these plans and put up some 3-4000 of this design. It was 28" long, 17" tall and 14" wide. It had a door way on the end of the box.

The problem with this configuration is that it allows the owls' mortal enemy, the crow, to see the owls inside the box as there is not a spot inside that is out of view. If crows find

The original configuration for the owl box with the hole at the end of the box.
Photo by Craig Hesse—Used with permission

owls during a daytime look in the box, they will use an alarm call that equates to the famous American call "To Arms!" It seems that barn owls eat crows on occasion. I have documented this only once, however. A flock of crows is called a "murder." This comes from the King's English as the black marauders would kill his hunting falcons if they were lost while out "hawking."

The owls are very conscious of whether or not predators can see them and will sometimes reject a nesting box of this design. By simply moving the doorway onto one side (rather than the end) of the box, I was able to give the owls all the privacy they needed without partitions and the like.

A branch for a perch was adamantly rejected by my local Audubon Society Chapter because of the belief that crows would supposedly use the perch to enter the box. I tested it for two years on my property and found that not to be the case with my design in a tree or on a pole.

The next thing that I found not to my liking with this box design was the clean out trap on the back of the box. I could not make the boxes out of thinner lighter material because it had to be thick enough to hold the screws that held the hasp and hinges affair on the back of the box. Also, I did not want my clients exposed to the yucky material inside the nest. The dust has a throat closing quality all its own. Besides, neophytes, well meaning or not, may decide to clean out the box at times when there is nesting activity. This is not a good thing at all.

I experimented with round doorways set up high on the left hand face. I found that for whatever biological reason, round doors attracted bees—it seemed within days—whereas the rounded rectangular doors did not attract them as much or as fast. Another difficulty with the high round door was that the box would fill up with pellets and other detritus. Soon the owls would run out of room to roost and nest. Hence, the need for a trap doorway for cleaning.

Ornate Owl Box

To deal with these difficulties, I elongated the doorway down to within an inch of the deck to allow the debris to slough out on its own. Turns out the female does housecleaning if given this configuration when nesting. This usually occurs just as the nesting season commences. I came home one day, got out of my truck and heard all this scratching coming from up in the "test tree." This tree is where I put all of my new products for testing. It is a scant ten feet from my garage.

The female was vigorously scratching inside the box, much like a chicken, but more vigorously. She was ejecting small clouds of dust, bones and pellets. This went on for some two hours then just as suddenly stopped. Like all bird behaviors, nest cleaning is set to mechanisms in their reptilian brains. Dinosaurs (birds) are a type of warm blooded reptile. Just look at the talons and scales on their legs.

I came to find that particle board is not a suitable owl nest box construction material. The waxy surface keeps paint and any anti-bee regimen application from adhering. In addition, most particle board products come apart when exposed to moisture. In the end I came to make the boxes out of a mahogany hardwood plywood. Hardwood-built boxes hold up to weather much better than coniferous laminates. Mahogany is strong and can be of a thinner ½-inch plywood because it is so strong. The doorway was now only the rounded rectangular type and cut on the best side for the owls privacy, opposite from the actual nest site or "scrape" and the female could clean it out when she desired. I was sensing some gratification in the design but I had one huge problem— bees.

Bees are easily attracted to owl boxes. They hang their combs from the ceiling, usually in a back corner. They find barn owl boxes very much to their liking and colonize the box whenever the fancy suits them. Wasps do as well in other parts of the country. Here in southern California, the insects would usually colonize the boxes in April—just when the owlets were just beginning to stand.

If the queen bee enters the box, the workers will defend her from any animal near her. This means that the owls must flee or die. Many died. I mulled over what to do about this problem for as long as I could bear. In time, I quit the owl box business altogether. I feared someone might get hurt, or worse.

In the interim, I had tried to repel the insects experimenting with many products to keep the bees out and keep the owls healthy. I tried oil, tobacco juice, even hot sauce to the ceiling inside where the bees would commence their honeycomb structures. Nothing worked. Dishwashing soap worked when applied to the ceiling but unfortunately it affected the owls when it rained. Then Africanized bees (sometimes referred to as "killer bees") moved into the region. That was it! I threw in the towel. For a year and a half I made and installed not a single box. All the while, it was my sad duty to take down boxes full of bees at much expense and frustration for me as well as my clients.

Over 80% of all unattended bee hives in San Diego and Los Angeles Counties are now Africanized crosses of the former docile Italian domestic feral bees. I am occasionally set aback when visiting a prospective client's property. They will often show me a "home made" nest box they installed without the anti bee stuff that has a resident colony of bees residing in the box.

The bees quite often have been tolerated there for years. I explain that if an Africanized queen bee fights and kills the residing Italian queen, it takes only a matter of hours for the hive to become aggressive. She tells them how they will now act.

I have had some clients pooh-pooh the threat these insects pose. I try to get through to them with "would you allow a rattlesnake to reside here with you in the garden? These bees are a threat to people and pets. If you install an owl nest box, you are responsible for the actions of any animals that reside in it, be they owls or bees.

Africanized bees are prevalent in a large part of barn owl habitat. All the lower states have these bugs or are about to get them. It is my understanding that zones of temperate climes have little problems with these insects there.

I have had some success with an application of WD 40 and fireplace ashes. I take the box and invert it so it rests on the roof. I then spray a layer of WD 40 on the inside ceiling and shake ashes on the WD and spread it around evenly. I then add another layer of oil and let the box set upside down this way for about 20 minutes to congeal the slurry.

Recent applications to the ceilings of a paintable Teflon product are showing promise as insects hooked feet cannot find enough texture to adhere to this product's surface.

After this experimenting I had a box that hung in trees. It had the doorway on the face, rather than the end, which allows the owls their privacy. It was bee proof. But I still had one big problem.

In those days all of the boxes were installed in trees, hanging by wires. Sometimes, it is not an easy matter for an experienced tree man to install these boxes. I have had more than one dicey moment installing them. As a disclaimer I do not recommend that the novice attempt to install the boxes in trees. Leave that to a professional—someone who is certified with the International Society of Arboriculture, like a certified tree worker or certified arborist.

Some of my clients did not have a tree high enough or in a suitable location. Sometimes their trees were too young or short. Some clients had no trees at all. Often the branches would break later after an installation. This is a set-up for disaster. If the branch breaks, it will then dump the contents of the box onto the ground. To try to prevent this from happening, I would secure the wires by a few jumbo sized staples or nails.

A barn owl box installed hanging in a tree.
Photo by Craig Hesse—Used with permission.

All the pine branches that I nailed into broke. This has to do with the biology of conifers. All conifers are made up of a suspension wood type branching structure. Just like a suspension bridge, pines and their kin keep their branches horizontal because their branches are held up by cells growing in series along the top of the branch. Any wound there would produce a failure of the branch in time.

I later found a particular looped chain to replace the wire that would grip the branch without a need to secure it with nails. The only problem I had now with this tree attachment was that the branch growth would grow over the chain or, "include" the chain. So if the box is put in a tree, a tree man needs to move the chains a little bit every two years or so to keep them from sticking in the new growth. This is best done in November as there is almost never any nesting activity during that month. It should be done a little earlier in colder more northern zones.

There were just so many tree logistics to work out. If only there was a way to mount the boxes on poles. At first I tried wooden poles. But I had a problem.

I had tried to mount the boxes on 4" X 4" wooden poles, concreted in the ground. I found that the wooden poles warped and predators, especially raccoons, could climb the poles. Even if the raccoon or opossum did not get all the way up and into the box, it still can startle an incubating owl off her eggs causing egg failure.

One day in Rancho Santa Fe, I was doing a walk-through of the garden area looking for a suitable spot to install a nest box. There was a large metal post in the center of a courtyard. The lady explained that her ex-husband used to put his flag pole in that and instead of taking the flag down every night, he would just take down the entire affair, pole and all.

The inside of this pipe was hollow and large enough to allow for my metal pole to be deposited inside with the nest box at the top. It was a simple matter of bolting the box to the 16' high metal pole and inserting it in the post. It looked kinda cool. There was something there. Some spark but I couldn't lay my finger on it. I went home gave it a thought or two but nothing came.

That night, completely asleep, I suddenly sat up in the dark and said to myself, "You dummy, put the pole OVER the post!" Come morning, I was at the fence supply store when they opened and I bought the

The author with his falcon, Brooke, and his barn owl nest box.

schedule 40, five-foot long, galvanized steel section of water pipe for a stand, and the 16' long 2⅜-inch pole and *voila, magnifique!* I installed it in my yard and got a barn owl, a male, in five weeks.

I have since installed nearly 25,000 boxes on this post and

The author and a Hoo's HOO box.
Photo by Sara Rosenbaum (Used with permission)

pole method. It is a simple design, because it is collapsible without being telescopic. The material is relatively cheap and usually available. When the post is driven into the ground sufficiently it is secure from falling over. It never rusts. It also paints well with a marvelous camouflage green paint product manufactured by Rust-oleum® solely for galvanized steel. (It works well on other surfaces as well.) This light matte green compliments the wood hue and dries in minutes.

I now had a product that looked appealing and could be installed in any yard or property in any location. But I had just one problem—sun and heat.

A nice gentleman client named Carlos Royal called one day and had me install a newly designed model owl nest box. I had recently met my new box maker, Rick Windle, and told him that I wanted a barn for our barn owls and so it was done. It was elaborate, equipped with an infrared

Fuzzy Owlets viewed on a monitor from inside the house
Photo by Robert Weigand—Used with permission

camera and therefore, more expensive so I named it after a book at the time about the well-heeled, entitled "Who's Who." The owner of a Hoo's HOO box could watch the owls in the box on their TV. I installed a "Hoo's HOO" for my client. However he had no shade trees as he lived in a new subdivision. Two years later, the box had an owl. The owl had eggs.

The client had a desire to share the experience with his mother (and later the world) and installed an internet camera onto the outside of the nest box. He and his wife,

Molly, The World's Most Famous Barn Owl
Photo by Carlos Royal—Used with permission

Donna, and the two avian inhabitants were internationally famous—seemingly overnight. They were blessed with some 20 million "hits" to their website in nine months, 34 million hits total.

I have spent hundreds of thousands of Federal Reserve notes on advertising over the years and the Royals just clobbered the market with $1200.00 worth of internet gear they bought at the local electronics depot. I was, to say the least, very impressed. They did all this with help from their grandson, Austin Faure, who was key in troubleshooting the bugs from the system during the year and a half broadcast. This was no small task, I can assure you.

It seemed as though the entire world was watching Molly and McGee in this box that I had installed. "Sweating bullets" is the phrase that described my anxious watching online every night. What if the nest failed? Everyone would take the assumption that this organic rodent control method does not work. I was proud of my little niche but I had not signed up for this.

But the endeavor led a charmed existence it seemed. Most clutches of eggs have an infertile or "addled" egg or two.

McGee and one of his juvenile female offspring
Photo by Carlos Royal—Used with permission

Theirs had only one. The other four eggs hatched and all thrived—praise the Lord. As the season advanced so did the temperature. As I mentioned, there were no trees. That the one box that went online had no trees for shade could only be chalked up to Murphy's Law. When I get to that great owl

A strategically placed ladder system provides the perfect, safe starting point for fledgling owlets.
Photo by Andrew Gepp—Used with permission

box in the sky I am going to have a word or two with this chap.

So now I install all of my pole-mounted boxes just to the east of trees if circumstances allow. This shades the nest from the hot afternoon sun. In addition, when the young fledge, they are tasked with returning to the safety of the box before sunup, or they could face many dangers. A free-standing A-

Owlet on a ladder, making its way back to the box with a rodent that had been dropped during transfer from the parent
Photo by Carlos Royal—Used with permission

Frame ladder that is the height of the doorway is recommended if there are not any trees immediately next to the box for the owlets to "branch" to. A ladder gives them a structure that they can use for short hop flights. If they end up on the ground, they can even "climb" the ladder to get back to the box, much the way they'd "climb" a tree. I place the ladder a few feet away from the box so as not to allow raccoons to leap onto the nest box.

Mr. Royal, in trying to provide plenty of fledging and branching opportunities, made additions and alterations to the box. Many of these proved ineffectual and were later removed. In his own words, "I would recommend that you leave the box like Tom built it."

Despite all my worry (and the worries of several hundred thousand viewers) the young in the Royals' box, although mildly uncomfortable from the afternoon sun, grew up as

Two fledgling owlets take refuge in a palm (Washitonia robusta)
Photo by Carlos Royal—Used with permission

expected and fledged without mishap. However, we encountered yet another problem.

When the chicks hatched, Molly pecked at the startled male and made him vacate the box to the banishment of the neighbors palm "tree" across the street. This was a surprise to me. In eighteen years of installing owl boxes I had assumed that they were both in the box, all lovey-dovey. It was of great concern to yours truly as, although thousands were watching, it seemed only I was aware that all the newly hatched youngsters could be in grave danger. I had another problem—crows.

The male owl, McGee as he was called, was somewhat secure from crows in his hiding place in the palm. But what if the neighbors decided to trim their palm? If that happened, the crows would eventually find him. If they did, McGee's chances of surviving an attack from a murder of crows would be slim, at best. If he were no longer around, the chicks would starve with everyone watching.

"Lions, tigers and bears. Oh my!"

The "his and hers" box
Photo by author

McGee surveys the surroundings of the residence he selected for his mate, Molly, and their young
Photos by Carlos Royal—Used with permission

This was all occurring at the height of the TARP banker bailout "recession." If the nest failed, I was envisioning the end of my only source of revenue, as humble as that was. Just in case, I went and bought a block of frozen mice at the pet depot store and had it ready.

When I learned that McGee was cast from the box as soon as the eggs hatched, I had my builder design a possible new box—a duplex or a "his and hers" box. It is, of course, much bigger and heavier and requires two poles for mounting (which means two men to install it). It is a viable solution to providing safe residence for both members of the mating pair (and perhaps their offspring, as well).

I have witnessed the successful human surrogate mothering of barn owls in their box without taking them to a wildlife rehabilitation permittee only once. This was done by another nice lady in the Pauma Valley Country Club years after my first install. She had both owl parents disappear .They were probably killed from eating rats that had been poisoned with rodenticides. This is termed being "secondarily poisoned." The half-grown young were starving to death. They had come to the point of cannibalizing each other. I was on vacation and was hundreds of miles away at the time but we put our heads together over the phone and worked out a solution to this new problem.

To her credit, this salt of the earth but well-to-do woman had the fiber to climb up a tall ladder every evening and dropped the prescribed amount of thawed out white mice in the nest box. She purchased these at the pet depot store.

This brave lady had absolutely no inclination to handle mice, dead or otherwise, but I talked her into doing what had to be done. She would thaw the mice out, put on her rubber kitchen gloves that hid her most beautiful diamond ring and with tongs in hand, climb up sixteen feet and toss the mice in. She managed to keep the young away from death's door. They fledged naturally on their own some weeks later. As you can see, over time and through much trial and error, I have found what I feel are the optimal design, installation and placement of barn owl nesting boxes. Others may disagree, but with almost 25,000 boxes successfully installed, I think I speak from the voice of experience.

An Ornate Box installed with a commanding view and nearby palm for shade and branching.

Chapter 4

Box Construction

Some aspiring owl box owners will build a nest box and then install it themselves. This is a trial and error experiment. Some homeowners do this and get owls the first season. Most do not. They make one or more errors in design or placement, causing rejection by the discerning owls, especially the females. One must build the right configuration of nest box, from the right materials and install the box correctly in the correct location.

If you are moderately familiar with woodworking it may suffice to build a simple nest box of a rectangular design. This model is 24 inches long and 15 inches high. The width is 13 inches, with a 20-inch deck or "porch" and a roof with an overhang at 16 inches.

The material is best made of hardwood laminates. I use Mahogany at a half-inch thickness, not Douglass Fir. Exterior grade Douglas Fir laminates do not hold up when exposed to weather for any appreciable length of time unless they are unusually thick— i.e., ¾-inch thick or more. This makes the nest boxes heavy and harder to install.

Basic Box Design
http://www.barnowlboxes.com/owl-boxes/basic-barn-owl-box/flypage.pbv.v1.tpl
Photo by Doug Sooley—Used with permission

Cedar is a good material but is hard to find in wide enough planks to fashion an owl box without an undue amount of boards incorporated into the building of the box. More boards show gaps. Cedar is usually overly thick and heavy. I have installed a number of cedar boxes produced back east by a popular nest box company that have a round doorway. These are found, in my opinion, to be made of good material, but the design and weight are not to my taste.

Because the doorway is set up high, the box needs to be cleaned (bad) and it has a round door that attracts bees and wasps (also bad) more often than an elongated doorway. There just seems to be no good way, either on a post or in a tree, to install this design. It's too bad, too, as I wish I could.

Box Construction

Whatever material you use, remember to keep the doorway to one side of the face of the box and not on the end. Only have a single doorway for each room space, not two and be sure the doorway comes close to the deck. This allows the female to clean the box when she desires. The doorways on my boxes are a 4.5" by 8.5" cutout, rectangular shape.

More experienced wood workers who wish to customize their nesting boxes have no limit to "cute" designs. My box maker excels at this. With added design input from me on what the owls prefer, my company has products that are presentable in any neighborhood. (*Please see www.barnowlboxes.com.*)

In site locations that are exposed to intense sun and heat, you may add a second layer of plywood to the outside of the box in a process known as "Fir out" or "Fir-ing out." This is adding 1' by 2" strips of wood, usually shop grade like fir around the outside of the box, near the edges of all the sides of the box. Then attach a second layer of plywood over that. This is to add a double wall to the box for insulation against debilitating summer heat. One might experiment with spray foam insulation inside, especially on the walls that are exposed to hottest part of the day and the roof.

Barn owls are a tough critters but the young suffer in temperatures over 100°F. During heat waves the young will leave the box and fall. Better that than to stay and die of heat prostration. See the "Box Placement" chapter on page 65 for further discussion of ways to protect the owls from extreme heat.

Maybe you are an organically minded farmer and intend to put these boxes out in the rows in full sun. If so, then yes, you should fir them out. Remember, barn owls do not often drink, getting all the moisture they need from the food they eat. So any undue loss of internal moisture through gular fluttering, which is like panting or "gaping," is critical. This is especially important to fledgling owls on the ground. Any handling of the owlets causes them great stress and loss of moisture through gaping and also excretion.

Another way to keep the owls cool is with ventilation. This needs to be done in a clever way and not by simply drilling holes in the upper areas of the walls of the box. This practice allows the owls to see out. If the owls see the enemies of owls, i.e. crows, they think the crows can see them, stressing the owls and changing their minds often as to whether or not they plan to stay. Sometimes they do, sometimes not.

Remember to emulate nature when and where you can. Barn owls typically nest in hollow trees. There is little in the way of windows there. These sites are off of the ground and are breezier than down on the ground. Birds can keep cool on hot days if they can get a breeze. Holes drilled in the pole will help air flow a little.

My fancier designs like the "Ornate" have spaces under the overhangs that allow for a breeze to flow through the box but yet does not allow the owls to see horizontally. I named this design when it was first built after an ornate hawk eagle (*Spizaetus Ornatus*) named Maya, which I was flying at the time. This species is arguably the most beautiful raptor.

Now add four holes on the bottom—one in each corner—for water drainage. Here in Southern California, ¼-inch holes are sufficient but you may want to make it ⅜-inch or larger in other parts of the world that receive more precipitation than here. Of course, do not make them large enough for the eggs to fall through.

Lastly a coat of paint or oil is good. Do not paint or oil the inside as you will need to add a bee deterrent later. The wood must be dry, clean and raw to absorb the oil. WD-40 and fireplace ashes do an adequate job of deterring bees.

Maya, the author's Ornate Hawk Eagle

Over half of all unattended bee hives in Southern California are now "Africanized killer bees." Many parts of South, Central and North America have these dangerous insects. The term "Africanized" means that they are an interspecific cross or (hybrid) between a wild African species of bee and a domestic Italian breed. This provides them with power and energy they would not normally possess called "hybrid vigor." This vigor, added with the ferocious defensive traits of the African line, makes putting up an owl box an endeavor not to be taken lightly.

Unless you are an experienced woodworker and have researched the construction of owl boxes, it is best to leave the construction to an expert. Likewise, unless you are a certified arborist or certified tree worker, it is also best to leave the installation of nest boxes in trees to the experts. There are just too many dangers inherent in installation to make this a job for an amateur.

Chapter 5

Box Placement

Of all the chapters in this book, this subject is the most diverse. You may have rodents and you wish to describe your property to me. Like snowflakes, no one property is like the other. You may live in Southern California as I do, or Texas. Maybe you reside in the Philippines or Bangladesh. Who knows? Barn owls live around the world and are arguably the most common owl worldwide.

What I am looking for when I visit your back yard, ranch or farm is a commanding view. I am not sure who or what they "command" but that is the dialect. This could be a view of an open field, or a gully, canyon or just a slope with more houses down on the next terrace. A nest box placed on a slope or high on a hill overlooking the owls' "foraging habitat" is ideal. I reject views obstructed by vegetation, structures and the like.

To use a well-worn saying, try to think like an owl. Imagine your arrival as you see the hoped-for box. Would you rather see it near the big tree, the barn or garage? Or would you, perhaps, prefer the fence looking out over an open area.

An open view will do no good, however, if the doorway has to face towards the hot afternoon sun. The owls will spend some time there in the box until one day the weather warms up perhaps. That is when the temperature gets above their comfort level and they go somewhere else to nest. I like to place the box just to the east of a tree for afternoon shade when available.

An open view is an open "lane" for the owl to approach the nest site. They will need to ferry in many a rodent making thousands of trips into the box. So we need to keep it clear and conspicuous.

Barn owls are somewhat "crepuscular." This means that they are most active in the twilight hours of dawn and dusk. In addition they often hunt at any time during the evening hours and need ready access to prey. For this reason they often nest on the edge of the forest bordering an open field. Bear in mind situating a box in such a place is not a hard and fast rule, but if possible, it is my advice. Other possibilities could be a canyon, gully, golf course or farm for example.

If you do not have an ideal spot, go for it anyway. When charted on a graph by biologists, all wildlife populations rise and fall due to environmental factors and biology. In peak years almost all the available nest sites will get a pair to inhabit the nesting box. A phrase I've heard often (less now here than I used to hear) is "it took a few years but we finally got a pair of owls nesting in the box." Good!

Box Placement

They will stay for generations if all goes well.

Some larger trees will suffice. As a disclaimer, I will reiterate—PLEASE do not attempt to install nesting boxes in trees. Leave that up to a professional certified arborist or certified tree worker. You will find one in your area by searching online for the I.S.A. You will need to tell him to hang the box by chains.

Try to find a branch that is strong enough to hold the weight of the box when full of soggy mashed up pellets including as many as ten baby barn owls (I have seen twelve) and their mother aboard. An east-west branch will point my designed box to the north which is what they

A box installed with plenty of shade and trees.
Photo by Lauren Greider —Used with permission.

prefer. So then, do I. Use a level on the roof and sides to get the owl house plumb and level.

If one cannot get a northward point to the doorway, then point the doorway any direction but towards the afternoon sun. If there are no obstructions like dwellings, hillsides and the like, Northwest to Northeast is best in this part of the hemisphere. Barn owls are like Dracula in this regard as they do not like the sun. A good rule of thumb a falconer taught me is "how would you like it?"

If you have a view of an open field to the east, let's say, then I might even forgo the northerly pointing of the box to direct it to this open expanse. Try to envision where they may hunt from at night. It's usually the same location that you could see hawks during the day perched up high. Same perch, different shift.

If you live in the far north (or far south) where it is much colder than mid North America, it may behoove you to turn the doorway east. Experiment with more than one box. Try different directions. once you get a pair of owls, note the direction they have selected. Try facing the boxes toward one another as the pair like to talk to each other after sunset and before they take wing. She often scolds him to get busy and bring some food. The two boxes could be both in trees, on poles or one of each.

Put up several boxes—either on your property or your H.O.A. The more boxes one puts up—the more you are enhancing barn owl habitat—the quicker you will get a pair of barn owls to inhabit one of the nest boxes. Their young,

Box Placement

after they fledge and disperse, usually take up residence in the vacant boxes.

In the average acre lot here in California, I like to put the boxes on the south side of the property. This way when I point the doorway northish, the owners can watch the face of the box. To say the converse, if I were to install the box on the Northernmost property boundary and point the doorway northish, the client would be looking at the back of the box. That is no fun as you cannot see the owls easily.

So the ideal spot would be:

1. On the south side of the lot.
2. Pointed northish.

A box with a beautiful view
Photo by Lauren Greider -Used with permission.

3. The ground slopes down and away to the north or is at least level.
4. Nothing is obstructing the view into the box and or coming up from under the box at the base of the pole like bushes, fences, houses, gazebos or vines growing up the pole, etc.
5. It is not close to someone's bedroom window.

I am fond of saying that there are four types of people near an active barn owl nesting site: people that hear them and those who do not. Of the first type, there are some who hear and don't really notice or care and then there are those people who like the sound that they make

A pair of fledgling female barn owls perched on a tree near their box.
Photo by Craig Hesse—Used with permission.

and those who do not. If you know someone of the latter type explain to them that the owls are eating and ridding them of their rodents as well. As a last resort, I counter with, "Did you make noise when you were an infant?"

To control rodents we have traps, poisons and barn owls. That's it. Take your pick and you will have a drawback. Who wants to handle trapped rodents? Not me. I particularly do not want poisons around my property and pets. My box is situated near my garage in a tree at the opposite end of the house from the master bedroom. I hear the male who calls when returning with a rodent occasionally. Just enough sound to let me know they are still around.

Barn owls emit a clicking call that is punctuated by a screech. The clicking can be heard by these birds at quite a distance. The screech note is no different. When a male suitor has taken up residency and is "soliciting" for a mate, he will click quite vigorously. So much so in fact that the nest box will be observed to quiver and shake. He is after all trying to prove to the female that he is indeed full of vigor and vitality. Humans are really not so different.

Eventually some unimpressed female will land nearby and call back, "Screech! Ok I am here, now what is it you want?" The male will amplify his calls and quicken their pace. Soon he will emerge from the box and fly closely past her. Here is when one can witness a natural delight. The courting flights of the common barn owl male.

He rises up spiraling over the female perched underneath, then "stoops," (the American pioneers' convolution of the word "swoops") down close by her. This will go on for a short while. When he is certain that she is watching, he will fly a straight line at full speed into the box calling mightily. This is the solicitation proper. "Come hither!"

If she enters, they will call to one another in a courting ritual millions of years old. Courting will ensue for anywhere from a couple of nights to a week ending in copulation. Therefore, because of these flights and to ensure successful courting and pair bond building, it is a good thing to have a nearby perch. This could be a tree, a pole or another nest box. This is not only for the female to come to call but for the male as well.

Another reason for a nearby perch is that when returning with prey for the female to feed the young, the male (and later both adult owls) prefer to land nearby on these perches. Then when it is ascertained that there are no threats from watching predators, they fly in and make a "prey item transfer." So, there is more to barn owl habitat than may meet the human eye.

There is a single pair in New Zealand as I write. A government biologist there answered my inquiry recently about whether or not the New Zealand government would like to see that population bolstered. He told me that barn owls are not effective in controlling rats! He may want to talk to the farmers in Israel. He mentioned further that they are not welcomed there because they are an introduced species.

He said the birds appeared not long ago, probably on a

ship. If they populate, they could be a detriment to nesting seabirds or some rare marsupial mammal. This is regrettable because there is a rat problem there, especially in the harbor district of Wellington, the capitol.

This danger to native fauna is also the case with the Hawaiian tern. Barn owls were brought to this enchanted island chain in the 1950s to control rats. The Hawaiian tern was not rare then and there was no act of Congress to protect them. In time the owls did control rodents as best that they could without a concerted effort to place nesting boxes for them. The terns suffered from human impact due to rats eating their young and their fish prey population reduction.

In time, the owls were found to eat an occasional tern

Hawaiian Terns (*Gygis alba*)
©Can Stock Photo Inc./gator—Used under license

chick. Nowadays, with an annual wild progeny in the dozens, a single juvenile mortality is a costly setback. This species of tern is a most beautiful fellow earthling.

Odds are barn owls are where you are or they used to be there. This species is in the top three most widespread birds in the world. All the earth's continents except Antarctica have or have had barn owls. Most islands have them as well.

Basically, anywhere there are rodents, there is some member of the genus "tyto." Rodenticides and habitat loss have done their skullduggery in extirpating this owl from some its usual haunts worldwide, like the Philippines. Now, with the barn owl

The author with his first Peregrine falcon
Photo provided by author

being un common there, this wonderful country is experiencing impact due to rats. The "cane rat" population has "gone biblical" and the rat population as a whole is not affected by rodenticides. The more cheap poison is used, the more newly hatched barn owl chicks die. So when the older breeding owls die off after their time is up, there is little recruitment.

Most widespread of the world's birds are the ravens, peregrine falcons and barn owls. These species are called "ubiquitous" or, ever present.

It is my hope, by means of you the reader, that this book will be a vehicle to re-populate the barn owl in areas where it no longer exists. The thought to convey this to you came to me recently as I drove North on the CA 805/I-15 overpass in San Diego. There I saw a female peregrine flying over her nest on a highway overpass. This species was all but written off as extinct just when I was old enough to legally trap my first one in 1969.

But a group of biologists, many of whom were past and future presidents of the North American Falconers Association, came together with a plan to captive breed a population of Peregrines here in the U.S.A. and release their progeny. This is The Peregrine Fund.

It sounds so simple. It was not, I can assure you. It is worlds easier to keep a failing population bolstered by vigilant conservationists that it is to bring back a population of a species of wildlife that has failed. Just ask the California Condor Recovery project. If it can be done with a world migrating carnivorous parrot, the peregrine, it can be done with the Common Barn Owl.

In states and regions where human impact has driven this

species' populations to the brink of non-existence, the property owners who want to control rodents there will need to bring the barn owl population back. Areas and states like Ohio, Michigan and Minnesota where there used to be a much larger population could build and install nest boxes on the fringes of the intact population and stretch it out north. Then it could go east and west from there.

Food, water and cover are all any given wildlife species needs.

A northern facing box recently installed for a client
Photo by author

The owls get their water from the rodents they eat so those two bases are covered, so to speak. All that is needed now is the roosting and nesting habitat or cover. The difference between nest boxes made of plywood though and their natural hollow tree nest sites is the insulation from the bitter cold of the Great lakes region that the thick wood of the trees provide. I have in my mind's eye a new dual "his and hers" nest box with deep insulation just for this project.

This project would need to be a concerted effort by resourceful individuals that come together to link up remnant populations to former habitat. The government has enough to do with managing their fiscal crisis without us citizens applying for yet more grants. Grants come from taxpayers. We need to solve this debt problem one owl box at a time.

Hootessa, an inhabitant of one of the boxes installed by the author
Photo by Katherine Bannister—Used with permission

For example, lets us presume that southern Ohio has the northernmost relatively intact population of breeding barn owls. Boxes placed strategically at the edges of this population and north from there interstate, could draw the owls back to once familiar valleys. Internet cameras installed in those boxes to monitor the data from the breeding owls will help with snap judgment calls needed to support the re-population effort.

With many individuals working together, we can bring back the populations of barn owls that once thrived in almost every region of the United States.

Owlet on left, "I am a piece of wood."
Owlet on right, "You lookin' at me??"
Photo by Craig Hesse—Used with permission

Chapter 6

Box Maintenance

Owl boxes get full of yucky stuff. I know. I have cleaned out hundreds of them. Remarkably these older boxes do not reek as one might imagine dead animals would. However, the material that comes out when cleaning the boxes does have a palate-closing property unique to this duty.

I never did like the thought of my clients coming into contact with the remains inside the owl boxes. Many sales hinged on whether it was to be the client or if it was going to be me that periodically would have to perform this duty. So in time I began to configure the boxes by elongating the doorway close to the deck, thus allowing the mother owl to clean out the box if given the chance. That made those discussions moot.

Besides, it is not ethical to disturb nesting owls for any reason. Without an internal camera, there is no way to determine if the owls are breeding or rearing young. One of the quietest but most delicate periods is when the eggs are being incubated. One never knows if they are in the box. Barn owls often lay a second clutch of eggs called the "double clutch," or the "recycle." They can still have young in the box as late as October.

Recently a lady friend of a client had mentioned that she had her gardener climb up on a ladder and look inside the box. There was an owl that was flushed out of the box at the first climbing and has not returned since. These owls go into the boxes for the cover the cavity provides. They stay in the box because they believe no predator has discovered them there. Once the owls have it in their head that they have been discovered, they are loath to re-enter. You may well imagine their fear of being trapped in the box with a predator blocking the doorway.

Having to incorporate the hinge and hasp affair to the clean out hatch on the back of some designs one might find on the internet, adds to the trouble and cost of construction, the thickness and thus the weight of the box and gives us humans another

A "self-cleaning" ornate box standing tall among the trees
Photo by author

needless chore. I would rather be drinking tea, a beer, or a glass of smooth Napa Valley red wine on a hot summer's day. I know, call me crazy.

Pellets, fecal material and urates as well as parasites could be in any nest box. The rodents that are their prey could potentially be a viral and or a bacterial hazard, as well. I am of the mind that the highly acidic digestive tract of all raptors has a cleansing effect on the pellet material. This notion is potential for yet another study. I have performed the cleansing of the boxes many times without the aid of gloves and particle masks and have yet to get sick. Do I recommend that you clean out the boxes without this safety gear? No, I do not.

So I do not recommend that you clean them out ever if it can be avoided. This is not possible with most other designs as the doorway is set too high on the face of the box or the end. I have designed my boxes so that there is almost never a need to visit them. Remember: "tender loving neglect." Owls, as I mentioned, are over 80 million years old and there has never been a human there to clean the nests out in all that time, so they do not need us to perform that duty now.

In the interest of my clients' feelings, I have removed a few dead chicks that were visible to the owners. Owl nest box owners must bear in mind that there will be new life. There will be some mortality, as well, especially with the young owls. I guestimate in my experience that the juvenile mortality rate to be on average about eighty percent. This is quite high, if not the highest, juvenile mortality rate of any native North American raptor. Ergo, it may take two clutches of young owls to produce a single breeding adult barn owl. If these survivors prove their worthiness to breed by persisting through their first winter, they will usually live a number of years, perhaps as much as nine or ten in some instances.

A "cookie" showing at least three years of pellets, masticated pellets, detritus, fecal material and urates.
Photo by Craig Hesse—Used with permission

Having some waste material, about 2½-inches of what I call "Barn Owl Shag Carpet," is actually beneficial. (Others have been known to call it "Gag Shag.") It is the natural duff that lines every barn owl nest. It consists mostly of pellets, which the female processes with her bill into a uniform layer. Over time multiple layers are stomped flat into a biscuit I call the "cookie." The cookie incorporates some animal remains, waste products and sometimes owl young that failed. I once gave a third grade student a cookie, which she dissected. She won 1st place in her school's science fair.

Barn owls do not import any material with the design to make or line their nests. The first year, they lay their eggs right there on the hardwood floor of the box and are quite unaffected by the elements. It's little wonder. After all, Emperor Penguins hatch their young on the tops of their feet in the harshest climate on this clinker, the third rock from the sun.

"Barn owl shag carpet" layer inside the box. This is an unusually high layer as the adult female died in the box for yet unknown reasons.
Photo by Craig Hesse—Used with permission

There is no need to add any material like wood shavings. This material could breed a slime mold that is an avian illness called Aspergillus. This fungi infects their air sacs or the avian equivalent of lungs. I have found some thought provoking items inside these boxes. Grass, weeds, beetle carapaces, half grown dead barn owl young, pigeon legs with pigeon club bands on them and entire crow skeletons.

One box, which had a known two clutches of young nest within in two seasons, had one hundred and two (102) rat tails inside. Bearing in mind that most rats are consumed whole, tails going "down the hatch" with the rest of the rodent, this leaves only the periods when the owlets are very young, that the tails are removed by the mother owl when tearing it up for her hungry chicks. Many a rat must have met its sudden end from this pair of owls.

If the prey or failed young are fouled and smelly, the parents usually take them far away at night. Where they take them is mystery. I have witnessed this behavior on many an occasion but have yet to find a single carcass. I like to think that they take them over to the neighborhood grump's property. All neighborhoods have one.

So let's leave the boxes and the owls within to their own devices as they would have us.

Chapter 7

Attracting Barn Owls

Once the property owner has built a nesting box of the correct design and material, and it has been installed in the best possible location, there is not much else to be done except install a second box—two boxes minimum. The second box is needed for the male to reside in for his cover.

You could install another box every five acres or so as dead reckoning—more if the rodent problem, in time, is not solved.

Some folks had a pair of owls and thought that all that was needed to be done. Owls can become satiated—especially when they first arrive. The "pickin's" are high in this target rich environment.

Female birds can run out of eggs after many years of nesting. This is termed being "egged out." They may live for quite a few years afterwards but produce no young. There is no great need to forage for food when she is egged out as there are no young mouths to feed other than the individual or its mate.

You can have owls and not have an end to rodent problems in this scenario. So have axillary boxes about the property or the neighborhood. Some of the young owls will invariably take up residence in them.

Having a few boxes around is a good attractant as it mimics the sections of riverbeds that hold trees that are hollow where nesting barn owls are sure to be found. Some trees are young, some mature and some are "old growth." These old growth specimens are the typical natural nest sites.

The first barn owl nest site I found was as a boy in the wilds of Sorrento Valley, CA. It was in a hollow Live Oak tree. There was a young owl there standing in the entrance. Later I measured the site it was 7' 2" from the ground. This is the second lowest nesting site I have yet witnessed. The first was in a plastic bucket on the ground, full of sand inside a Sea Train storage trailer on a ranch in Temecula, CA.

I took this bird home with me. Hey, it was 1965 and no-one cared. It was not so long before then that owls and hawks were viewed as "vermin" to be shot on sight. I took him everywhere with me all that summer, riding around in the basket of my bicycle, playing on the lawn chasing stuffed toys on a string.

I fed him rodents that I trapped with snap traps I had set out in the fields and gophers trapped in my lawn. This is where I learned how to trap rodents as any shortcomings in his diet were purchased with my paper route money. I said,

"To heck with that." Why buy rats at the pet store when rodents are everywhere?

In time he learned to fly and learned to catch his own food. I would walk down the sidewalk and he would follow me screeching for food and company. On these walks at times he would venture some distance away, I would reward him with a mouse for this behavior.

By back to school time, he was completely at liberty and sleeping all day in the trees in my backyard. Come night he would land and screech just outside my window knowing my particular quarters. Just like semi-feral ranch cats farmers have, I would feed him not quite enough to sustain him, which is what occurs in a crèche about this season of the year. This was all the motivation he was lacking. He began to not show up as often, having caught his own prey. Then by Christmas he disappeared to be a barn owl with the thousands of other barn owls. This is an age old falconry practice called "hacking back." What tales he must have had for his new wife.

It could take years to cap a large population of rapidly reproducing rodents for a single pair of barn owls to control. More boxes mean more owls which mean more competition for food and cover, less rodents.

Some observers comment that some owls do not forage as far when there are other pairs nesting nearby. Maybe that is because they can keep one eye on the prey and one on their mate.

A female owl recently learned to enter my pigeon loft at night through the one way doors called "traps." This owl has been nesting for years in my Sycamore tree, the "test" tree. I took down her old dilapidated nest box recently and installed a new box with a web camera inside.

For two weeks I would check it periodically and no owls. Then I noticed a downy "type two" feather waving in the slight breeze on the floor of the box but no owl. Next day I put a pigeon that she had killed recently in my loft in there.

As I type these words I am watching her consume a "full gorge" as in falconry jargon. So I have attracted her to spend some time in this new and strange box with food. But this method is not recommended as re-entering the nest box to clean out the leftovers and put fresh rodents there would frighten away any new inhabitants if there were no camera.

Again, it's tender loving neglect. Leave the box alone. You should get owls. If this doesn't happen quickly, try not to get anxious—it takes longer that way. They will come when they come. Ask any turkey hunter about bird time. Birds are not on our scheduled agenda. Barn owls are on "owl time."

 Be observant for the expected inhabitants. One need not actually see or hear the owl to know that there is one inside the nest box. Subtler signs may indicate their presence. A bit of down stuck to the wood grain of the doorway for example. On a calm warm morning you might see a fly buzz in and out. This means there is fecal material inside. If you see streaks of white droppings or what I call "liquid rats" on the roof, you probably have an owl inside, maybe two. They perch there on top of the box at night.

A stylish stucco house that had barn owls nesting in the Terra Cotta pipe holes in the walls.
Photo by author

Some power poles are more dangerous to birds that others.
This is an extremely hazardous specimen.
Photo by author

Chapter 8

Electrocution

Birds are especially vulnerable to electrocution on power poles, power lines and those grey canisters called "transformers." Once the bird lands on the wooden pole, it is grounded. If any part of the bird then touches an energized power line, that bird is done for. Many wildfires – fires that have killed people—are started by the burning bodies of birds falling to the ground.

An electrocuted dead adult barn owl
Photo by author

Once near Pyramid Lake, Nevada, I worked as an assistant to a gifted falcon breeder. While there, I noticed smoke rising from the grass on the uninhabited north side of the property. Quickly I filled a bucket with water, but by the time I arrived at the blaze, the water was too little too late.

If I had run back to the house at this time to get a shovel, the fire would have grown so large before my return it could have possibly burned the valley with its homes. I was forced to stamp out the growing circle of flames with a crazy dance. Stomping with my left foot on the burning line of fuel, I kicked the already burnt black ground back onto the ring of fire with my right foot, all the while going around and around the perimeter as fast as possible. I call it the world's first crossfit "rep" or exercise. Had there been any wind, it would have been unmanageable. It took fifteen minutes of this wild corraboree but I succeeded in extinguishing the flames. I was exhausted afterwards. At the center of the charred area was a very dead, electrocuted falcon.

I have witnessed a number of dead golden eagles, hawks and falcons killed from power line execution. Many raptors are killed every day from electrocution in America. However not many are reported as there is a coyote clean up committee every night.

I have seen raptors, notably some very special and beloved falcons that had lived through attacks by golden eagles, other hawks, coyotes and impacts with vehicles only to be BBQ'd before our very eyes. Falcons are especially vulnerable to the grey canisters with the two squiggly wires emitting from the top of the can.

Harris's Hawks are susceptible to electrocution by their unique biology. These are the only social raptors in North America. They hunt in close knit groups that mimic alpha dominated wolf packs. Two birds flying side by side have a combined wingspan large enough to kill both birds. These are usually the dominant female and her daughter as they are the largest of the two sexes. This is a catastrophic calamity for the flock or "troop" as they are often referred to.

San Diego Gas and Electric employee removing the electrocuted owl. NO citation was ever written.
Photo by author

These birds are otherwise so tough they are able to live their entire lives without drinking water in the Sonoran Desert heat.

Larger birds of prey like golden eagles are vulnerable because their wingspan is so large it can span the wires or "cross phase." I did this to myself with an extension pruner while working as a tree trimmer back in the mid-1970s. I am very lucky to be alive, having escaped death by the slimmest of margins. This seems to be par for my life's course as I

Barn Owl in Flight
Observe the wingspan—approximately 42 inches (107 cm)
Photo by Craig Hesse (used with permission)

inadvertently make a habit of this sort of thing. You may see an example of a hawk being electrocuted by watching the video "Raptors at Risk," produced by the North American Falconer's Association.

My family has taken my dedication to raptors with some lack of understanding or some degree of disinterest, but there was one owl, a Eurasian eagle owl (*Bubo bubo*). He alone was loved by my wife and daughter. As this huge owlet emerged for the first time from his shipping crate onto our lawn, he was quite a surprise to them with voluminous down flowing about in the breeze. My daughter thought him "Puffy," so indeed he was. "Puffy" was a family pet that went with me everywhere for the next four years. He accompanied many a nest box installation.

Puffy would play about the crew cab of my pickup, then lie

"Puffy" the Eurasian Eagle Owl as a larger fledgling.
At this point he weighed about four pounds.
Photo by author

down to rest on my lap as I drove like some meter long incubating chicken. I never trained him to hunt as is the regimen for other falconry birds as Puffy was slated for education. Once a wind storm, common in the town I live in, tore the hinges off of Puffy's chamber, or "mew." He flew off into the night.

Four days later I found him sleeping on an abandoned rabbit hutch, of all places, and brought him home. Soon I found him to be a changed bird psychologically. He was never again content to ride about untethered in the truck. After his taste of freedom, he would constantly try to escape. Soon, just like a later Harris's Hawk I possessed, he became an "escape artist." Most everyone has known a neighborhood dog that has found out it likes life "on the outside" and how to get there. So it was with Puffy.

Puffy, in repose
Photo by Les Blenkhorn
Used with permission

Puffy puffed up in threat display as a dog ran up next to the author as he took the photo.

A couple of months later I opened the mew door and he shot past me and flew down into the riverbed trees some blocks away. He was officially AWOL. I searched for him all the next day and most of that night. The following day, I painted big signs that read "Lost Owl —Reward." I had just put the first nail in one sign to display it when a school bus driver stopped and said that the owl was in his freezer at work.

Upon salvaging the carcass, his feet were found to be charred. The driver said it was found at the base of the power pole at his work. I later had him mounted and he has accompanied me on many educational talks. I should have done this with all of my deceased raptors. They are educational in death as well as alive.

The next day, I called the San Diego Gas and Electric claims representative. I asked the rep to please pay the $4,000.00 re-reimbursement for my dead owl and I would let the other moneys I had spent on him ride. He laughed at me!

The power pole that killed Puffy, owned by San Diego Gas and Electric, a SEMPRA company.
Photo by author

San Diego County suffered the biggest wildfire in California History to date back in the year 2007. This was like no other fire this native had before witnessed. Called the "Witch Fire," it advanced at speeds up to 100 MPH. It consumed brush, trees and over a thousand homes and houses. This blaze tore through this region and killed sixteen people. The fire was started by loosely strung power lines touching one another. The resulting sparks igniting this firestorm.

During the next few months the local power company re-erecting the grid had the unique opportunity to install a cheap piece of plastic on each power line called "bird guard." They elected not to do this. No such device was installed then. Thousands of lines went back up with numerous raptor mortalities due to electrocution occurring since then. These raptor deaths could have easily been prevented.

If you or I were to shoot a raptor, perhaps in the defense of our livestock, or as a raptor propagator simply fail to send in the paperwork on captive bred raptors in a timely manner, we would run the gauntlet of the U.S. Judicial system. How is it that monopolistic power companies and other corporations can, all in the name of profit, kill thousands of raptors nationwide through electrocution or being chopped to pieces by the rotor blades of "green" wind farms, without having to pay one dollar in mitigation? Perhaps the US Fish and Wildlife Service and the judicial system needs to consider a more preventative and common sense approach to the enforcement of the Migratory Bird Treaty Act[1] and consider fines and

---

[1] For further explanation and discussion of the Migratory Bird Treaty Act, see Chapter 13, page 97.

A power pole configuration with hot lines insulated properly with "bird guards" going in two directions, one above and one below. Located one block from the San Diego Safari Park (formerly the San Diego Wild Animal Park).

punishments for utilities, oil drilling and logging companies who fail to take necessary steps to avoid preventable deaths of raptors and other migratory birds. While some deaths really are accidental and unpreventable, many others could be avoided through the implementation of some simple and inexpensive measures.

Until such measures are commonplace, it is up to concerned bird lovers to do what we can to protect our avian friends. Once you install a barn Owl nest box, it may behoove you to call your power company to inspect the lines nearest the box. You might also ask them if they will install bird guards on the lines around the area.

Female American Kestrel
Photo by Craig Hesse Used with permission.

Chapter 9

Kestrels

This book is about barn owls and how to build and install nesting boxes to attract them. However there exists another species of highly beneficial raptor. Kestrels are found around the world and eat hundreds of pounds of rodents and insects every year.

Although not as easy to attract as Barn owls, it is worth a try.

Suburban back yards are usually not conducive to attracting these fine falcons but if the property is abounding a field or high on a hill, some properties can and do have kestrels about.

American kestrels are beautiful little falcons. They weigh just a few ounces. They are dimorphic, which means that the sexes differ in plumage. The male is red, white and blue. The female has a buff belly and brick red plumage with dark barring on the top half.

These feisty little falcons do not seem to be aware they are small, projecting an aggressive attitude badge wherever they go. Kestrels are usually seen flying around fields and hillsides, calling their high pitched cry announcing their presence, "Killy Killy Killy." To me as if to say "you (another hawk) better not be there, 'cause if you are- you're gonna get it right now!" They can often be observed harassing or "harrying" a Red Tailed Hawk. This is where the name Harry comes from, the days of yore of Olde England.

When foraging for a meal, kestrels are most recognized as the hawk that hovers. Hovering is a flight adaptation for hunting earth-bound prey. In flight they will move up to position themselves over an area of ground to be inspected then stay stationary by rapidly fluttering their wings. Although their body is shaking vigorously when engaged in this activity, their head and more importantly, their eyes are perfectly immobile. They are the first spy satellite. Terrain viewed from above in this fashion is scanned for any movement by rodent, bug or twitching grass.

A kestrels drops down from a perch or a hover into the vegetation and pluck some hapless victim. He often has it consumed before he alights on the branch of a dead tree or a pole. I once had a kestrel named "Egor." Egor was at hack, or at liberty, to come and go as he pleased. Brother Bob and I were in a vigorous rally of ping pong and this falcon was on the television antennae above us. Egor dropped down just above the table as if to grab the ping pong ball but continued into the freshly mown grass and smartly grabbed some bug so small we could not see it from ten feet away. "He eats germs!" exclaimed Bob. It was probably a gnat.

Kestrels and virtually all birds have inherited the world's keenest eyesight. All of my life, I have searched for the

A male American Kestrel that made his home in an owl box.
Photo by Craig Hesse—Used with permission

proper assemblage of words to successfully convey to you how good a hawk's eyesight is. Suffice to say, it is a natural wonder. Kestrels and all other birds can see almost the entire light spectrum. We are limited to the center of that range. Birds can process images in a fraction of the amount of time that we lowly mammals are able to. Called "flicker," it is how much time passes for the light photon takes to get from point A to point B- from retina to brain. Birds called "skimmers" have the fastest reaction time known, snapping shut their beak upon touching a fish when unzipping water surface tension.

Thus Kestrels can see, among other things, urine that is deposited by rodents along their paths through the grass. This is one way these mammals communicate with one another. Any accumulation of these urates shows up as a bright iridescent to these predators. These are the areas that get most of the hovering attention. If you have heard the ancient falconry jargon that this person "just hovering over" him or her', kestrels' flight is where we get this phrase. Other birds of prey, from golden eagles to Kingfishers hover as well.

Kestrels can be attracted to a nest box that is the proper size and with a doorway that is just big enough for the female to enter. The male can fit into most any doorway a female is able to. Kestrel boxes and their doorways are perfect also for Screech and other small owls. Kestrels have even been known to, at times, nest in barn owl boxes.

A box specifically designed to meet the needs of nesting kestrels.
Photo by author

American Kestrels, at home in their "owl box"
Photo by Craig Hesse—Used with permission

In Arizona there are a number of species of screech owls that have been impacted by human activity for the last century to the point that few persist in the wild. This due to the fluctuation of river levels and other factors. This fluctuation is a detriment to stands of native trees like Arizona Cottonwood (*Populas fremonti*) in which they nest. When or if the opportunity arises, I would enjoy building and installing boxes for those species someday, a nest box is just as good as a hollow tree.

A owlet who appears to be shy but is actually scratching its head
Photo by Colleen Gepp—Used with permission.

Chapter 10

Natural vs. Chemical Rodent Control

In the recent past, rodent poison was made of lethal compounds that were so effective, some were billed as "one-bite" as that was all that was needed. The rodents would ingest the poison; thrash around for some time before succumbing. In their death throes is often when a hungry owl would see the affected rodent as food (which they normally would be) eat the rodent and be "secondarily poisoned."

Newer poisons are of the blood thinning type, which are decidedly less lethal. The thinking being that the rat has to visit the bait station frequently for a few nights or so in order to accumulate enough poison internally to bleed to death. The unlucky owls that ate an occasional dying rodent would in turn, have to eat a number of rodents at that level of toxicity to die itself.

This is better than the one-bite bait, but adult owls do die on occasion from the blood thinner poisons. Just ask your raptor rehabilitation facility if they get poisoned birds of prey. While you're on the subject ask them if they ever get any ill raptors that have ingested lead bird shot.

Prospective clients often call and say they have a "terrible

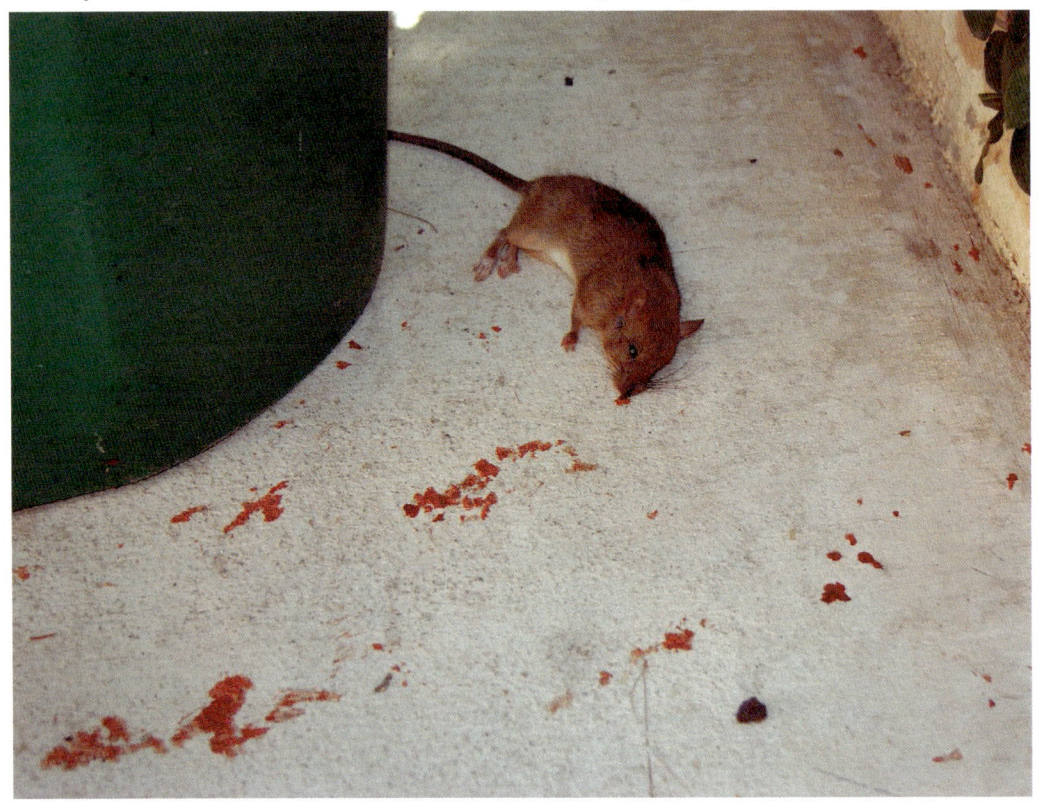

A rat killed with blood-thinner poison. Note the droplets of blood from its thrashing about in death throes. This attracts owls and other raptors.
Photo by author

rat problem." I remark "oh, you use rodenticides." They think I am clairvoyant. It is my take that for one, poisons do kill some rodents, but as a effective rodent control method, it is lacking, making the infestation worse, in my humble opinion.

Here in suburban Southern California, every neighborhood has a pair of barn owls living somewhere, usually in an untrimmed palm "tree" (palms are not trees, they have a common ancestor with corn, rice, stoloniferous grass and bamboo called "monocotyledons"). These may not be the best

Natural vs. Chemical Rodenticides

nest sites but the owls are often successful there and produce some young. It is when these birds are destroyed that the real rodent control is removed. That is when rodent populations "go biblical'.

After decades of observation and taking into account my years of breeding hawks (raptor propagator) I will make my case.

Communities will use rodenticides as the primary rodent control method. The owls are sickened and leave, especially where it is policy over a wider neighborhood like home owners associations. Those owls that stay, feed their young poison laced rodents. The young die as they are many times

Natural Rodenticide
From the movie *Back Yard Barnowls*
Photo by Bert Kersey—Used with permission

A curious owlet looks on as her sibling devours a rodent.
Photo by Colleen Gepp—Used with permission

more affected by the poison than are the adults.

I know from years of incubating raptor eggs that if you have anything go wrong during the process, the newly hatched hawk or falcon or owl, in this case, lets you know something was done wrong by dying. They start life as a tiny spark and need nurturing. Any little bit of impact and life goes out.

The owl population in the study area do not produce any recruits due to the poisons used and the adults eventually pass on. Now there are no owls present. The mice will play when the owl is away.

Further, there are codes of conduct we humans live by. One is civilized people do not let innocent animals suffer unduly.

Why is it that we can spread these toxins around as if they are confetti, letting rodents and other wildlife suffer a prolonged agonizing death? There are other laws that restrict much less abhorrent behavior to animals. Rodenticides are

Rodenticides are dangerous to cats, dogs, and other domesticated pets, as well as children, local wildlife or livestock. Any of them can be poisoned through secondary poisoning by consuming or handling poisoned rodents.
© Can Stock Photo Inc./marcovarro —Used under license

justified somehow. The state of California has a website that catalogues the species of animals that have been known to be secondarily poisoned, listed from A to Z. The first subject starts with "children."

In any event, one needs to remove rodent bait before putting up the nest box. Switch to snap traps. They make them in containers just like the rodent bait stations. This so that children and pets are not injured. Bury these dead animals that are caught in the garden as well.

Worm food is worm food, no matter the compost source. Worms are the node in the communities of life that live around the hair like "feeder" roots of trees and plants. Without these humble servants, most landscape vegetation suffers.

The Ramona Grasslands Preserve.
Photo by Craig Hesse—Used with permission

Chapter 11

US Law Regarding Migratory Birds of Prey

Birds of prey (raptors) have been highly prized since before recorded history. Known as "the Sport of Kings," falconry is the world's oldest known field sport. The tomb of Chinese Emperor's Qin Shi Huang yielded a book of water color paintings of the emperor doing many royal things.

On one page the monarch is portrayed tying a trained Goshawk to a screen perch, just like the screen perch falconers use today, minus all the silk and gold, of course. The researchers' thinking was at the time that he was the most pampered man in the universe. He certainly was not subsistence hunting. He went "hawking" for sport. The knot depicted in the painting, the falconer's knot, is, ergo, the world's oldest documented knot according to *National Geographic* magazine. I have had sailors argue the point. "Ok- prove it," I counter . So far, their only answer is silence.

No doubt, those knots sailors tied got falconers to distant lands to procure hawks for their sport. In medieval Europe, a handful of ships were sent by King Frederick II, Holy Roman Emperor, to the North Sea for the purpose of providing the crowned heads with white gyrfalcons. Ships were lost, many men died but some returned with a hand full of these the largest of all and most magnificent falcons. Two white gyrfalcons once were traded to a King's captor for his release. These two birds were literally worth a "King's Ransom."

Falconry was practiced by primitives and royalty before recorded history. As the famous American ornithologist, Roger Tory Petersen said "Man emerged from the mists of time with a peregrine on his fist."[1] Yes, indeed he did. I might add that he was riding a horse and a dog trotted alongside. There are two tribes of herdsmen in Mongolia that have flown golden eagles at hares, foxes and wolves, probably since the polar caps melted ending the Pleistocene epoch. That would be one way to "keep the wolves at bay."

Falconry was brought to Europe ostensibly by Marco Polo, where it enjoyed its greatest heyday as the "Sport of Kings." More recently wild Alaskan peregrine falcons were traded by the U.S Government to sweeten oil deals with Persian Gulf royalty in the 1970's. This was being done at a time when the Federal government was in the process of listing the American peregrine as "endangered."

Raptors are held in such esteem by commoners and heads of state alike that our governments have signed treaties protecting them when they migrate across borders. International treaties are the highest order of the United States, superseding all personal and private property rights. After all, down through time, international treaties that were broken, caused wars.

Would we as a nation go to war if some other nation trapped or killed some of our native raptors? Hardly. Nonetheless, this is the

---

[1] This statement is used by Mr. Peterson, with similar wording, in many of his books.

US Law Regarding Migratory Birds of Prey

Friend of the author, Gary Boberg, and his stunning White Gyrfalcon.
Photo by Becky Boberg—Used with permission

level of protection afforded the barn owls and their carnivorous cousins. The raptors alone are claimed by our Federal government to be its property. You or I cannot pick up a feather of a raptor that you find on a hike or in your back yard without a permit.

I won't lie and say that I agree with the enforcement of the MBTA and the fact that captive bred raptors are the property of the government and not the breeder, but, supposedly, the intent of the law was originally positive. Prior to the passage of the "Migratory Bird Treaty Act," or MBTA, it was common practice to hunt non-game birds. Many wild, typically non-food birds such as Bobolinks and Cedar Waxwings were served as delicacies in restaurants and women even adorned their hats with stuffed baby birds. Many people collected wild bird eggs as a hobby and some bird watchers and ornithologists actively collected specimens of rare birds instead of just recording the sighting. The MBTA's original purpose was to protect native birds from such activities. In practice, however, things are not always as they were intended. The current overreaching enforcement of the MBTA is one such example.

Here in the U.S, barn owls and all raptors are classified as "Migratory Birds," protected by the MBTA[1]. Even raptors and other birds that do not migrate are considered to be "migratory" like barn owls under the provisions of the MBTA.

Brooke, the Spanish peregrine
Photo by Stephen Ford—Used with permission

I once had a female captive-bred Spanish peregrine named Brooke who the US Air Force hired, with me as her trainer, to clear USAF runways. I had other offers to perform bird control at county airfields and in the private sector such as wine grape vineyards. After inquiring for a special permit to allow me to work in the private sector, I was told that although there are provisions to allow captive bred raptors in a for profit venture, the federal government was not issuing any permits "at this time."

Later I found out that it was because my non-native, non MBTA Spanish peregrine could not be used in the private sector simply because she looked like a native peregrine! They cited some "similarity clause." Whatever.

US Law Regarding Migratory Birds of Prey

Barn owls are very beneficial directly to humans and as such are extremely valuable as wild creatures because of their appetite for rodents. If you have a bad rodent problem, it is due to the lack of barn owls. Put your hand on the radio, Amen.

The message here is there are stiff penalties for possessing any raptor without a permit, even captive bred raptors. To put this in context, one can possess, breed, slaughter for meat and hides, captive bred elk, deer, bear and many other mammals and birds, they being the owner's property. Not so birds of prey. The US Government claims ownership of them alone.

Captive bred raptors are considered the property of the breeder for whatever purpose he wishes in all but a few other nations. But not here in the U.S. Permits are needed and that is almost always a falconry permit. A falconry permit is a lengthy and arduous task. Study, examinations, licensed sponsors, money and time are prerequisite for such an endeavor. Falconry is the most highly regulated hunting sport in America.

So when you see a fledgling barn owl about the nest box, respect the law and the wildness of the animal. It is where they get their beauty. Until this law is changed to allow for domestication of barn owls, view them on TV or on internet live-streaming..

[1]The original 1918 statute implemented the 1916 Convention between the U.S. and Great Britain (for Canada) for the protection of migratory birds. Later amendments implemented treaties between the U.S. and Mexico, the U.S. and Japan, and the U.S. and the Soviet Union (now Russia). Specific provisions in the statute include: *Establishment of a Federal prohibition, unless permitted by regulations, to "pursue, hunt, take, capture, kill, attempt to take, capture or kill, possess, offer for sale, sell, offer to purchase, purchase, deliver for shipment, ship, cause to be shipped, deliver for transportation, transport, cause to be transported, carry, or cause to be carried by any means whatever, receive for shipment, transportation or carriage, or export, at any time, or in any manner, any migratory bird, included in the terms of this Convention . . . for the protection of migratory birds . . . or any part, nest, or egg of any such bird." (16 U.S.C. 703)*

Two bright eyed fledglings. No poisons, chemicals or lead shot.
Photo by Craig Hesse—Used with permission

Chapter 12

Orphaned Owlets and Injured Owls

These are good examples of how to co-exist with wild owls. Once habitat is provided, the care extends as far as "tender loving neglect." Please do not touch or approach wild owls. Leave them be. They are not pets.

Often the owlets are found standing on the ground. The average homeowner assumes that something must be wrong. They are

Do not handle fledglings. It is stressful for them as they lose hydration.
Photo provided by author

Owlets that leave the nest too soon often face increased danger from predators.
Photo by Colleen Gepp—Used with permission

indeed vulnerable there. This is one of the most dangerous times in every owl's life, in a backyard or out in the woods.

Although not all fledglings end up on the ground, some do. This is quite natural. So is owl mortality. Be prepared for this mentally when you endeavor to attract barn owls, especially with the juveniles as they occasionally pass away for one reason or another.

Barn owls have one of the highest juvenile mortality rates in the world of raptors. Mortality is part of Darwin's selection theory. Natural selection is how vigorous owls that are full of vitality persist and breed in the nest box.

If death occurs, bury them in the garden and plant something there. From death comes new life every time.

These temporarily terrestrial birds appear as if tranquilized during the day and just stand there with their eyes all squinched up. That is what I call the "never mind me, I am just a piece of wood" look. Instinct tells them to just stand still.

You may cautiously take some photos from a distance of about thirty feet if you wish, even using the flash. Keep any dogs or other pets away for the day if possible. I have never heard of a cat attacking a fledgling owl but I would not put it past a pedigree Siamese breed.

As a young lad I, when was pedaling my way to the beach, I saw a Siamese cat that was owned by an Asian fellow. He was a professor at Scripps Institution of Oceanography. He had the cat on a long chain in a vacant lot and I went to pet it. The owner shouted a warning and I stopped. The feline assassin was stayed by the end of the chain at eye level, a scant six inches from my face. It made a frightening sound as it did so. The professor explained that Siamese were bred to protect temples. This was one of the working individuals.

If you find the owls have something obviously wrong with them, then by all means call a licensed wildlife rehabilitation facility. Inquire as to their contact information through your state wildlife agency. It is a good idea to contact one which specializes in birds of prey beforehand. "An ounce of prevention is worth a pound of cure."

Do not feed the owls or confine them. This is not so say that they may not be hungry. Leave care and handling to the qualified individual.

The author at the Southern California Exposition (AKA the "Del Mar Fair) with a human imprinted, non releasable barn owl owned by Project Wildlife San Diego. raptor rehabilitators.
Photo by Charles Gilband —Used with permission.

Chapter 13

Domestication of Barn Owls

For approximately the last ten thousand years, mankind has taken wild animals out of their native environment and domesticated them for food and company. From cattle to cats, chickens, dogs, horses, goats, pigs, sheep, pigeons and even fish have been bred for thousands of generations to suit our fancy. Falconers cross breed falcons today and are in the most human process of creating *falco domesticus*.

Recently the breeders of birds of prey, called "raptor propagators" have bred a few dozen barn owls here in the US and in Europe. Mankind would benefit greatly to have domestic barn owls living in their dwellings with them, especially in poorer countries. And

Male barn owl in flight
Photo by Steve Chindgren—Used with permission

why not? Look how our lives have benefited by the keeping of other domestic animals.

With construction providing proper sanitation measures and an access doorway like a flapping pet door, your attic could become a barn owl roost. A rat would only need to enter there and his life would be dispatched post haste.

With a little education and some store bought frozen white rodents from a pet store/depot, barn owls would make great pets. There is a famous book about an American biologist who rescued one and kept him as a pet.

I have had several barn owls and they were very entertaining and educational. I loved them greatly but in a different way than my hunting falcons and hawks. Mine lived inside a cage (mews) sleeping there during the day. They were released each night to be a wild owl for as long as the darkness lasted.

Captive male Barn Owl. A potential breeder for domestication.
Photo by Steve Chindgren—Used with permission

With the addition of a one way door on the mews such as pigeon fanciers' "traps," the owls could return each morning for a treat and some shut eye, then be released at dusk to hunt rats, mice and gophers (if you've got them). It would be the best of both worlds. Domestic barn owls kept throughout neighborhoods would do very well to control rodent populations in a way that no trapping regimens or rodenticides could come close to managing.

Barn owls could be selected for whatever traits the keeper wished to see. Hunting traits, wild coloration, white factor, whatever. Cold or heat tolerant traits could be managed just like is being done with arctic gyrfalcons kept by royal families in the oil rich Arab Gulf regions today.

Barn owls, wild or domesticated, are not a threat to people. They are about as dangerous as a common house cat. While loose, they might, of course, occasionally eat a songbird. Some people would have something to say about that, but it needs to be emphasized that this is the nature of things.

Island archipelagos like Hawaii would not be the place to introduce such a non-native intruder but the entire American continent, especially in suburbia, would benefit greatly. The rodent pest problem is bigger than the negligible impact to wild species as the barn owls specialize in rodents almost exclusively.

If some wildlife species were to become rare for whatever reason, pollution, habitat loss, that species should be captive bred by a re-introduction and habitat saving organization. There are models for this with the Peregrine Fund and Ducks Unlimited. The Peregrine fund has pioneered the captive breeding and re-introduction of Peregrine Falcons and other raptors on a large scale. Ducks unlimited has moved mountains in their quest to preserve and enhance waterfowl breeding and foraging habitat and to bring waterfowl populations back from the brink of extinction. Both entities bolstering populations of these once rare birds to the point that management is becoming necessary.

Decades of proven track records by this club have shown the way to successful grassroots conservation. This conservation costs pennies on the dollar that a federal government agency would spend. Such an agency would be paying for the effort by taxing us yet further and doing a lackluster job of conservation, to boot. Government taxation and over regulation are a log jam in the way of the free market river, so to speak.

As the federal government has declared that they, not the U.S. citizens, are the owners of barn owls, the effort to wrest ownership away from the "feds" and back to the rightful owners would take some lobbying in Washington. But it is worth it. After all, we are talking about ownership of CAPTIVE BRED birds.

What impact on the wild owl resource would captive bred owls have on populations as gigantic as wild barn owls? The captive genes would be swallowed up by the wild pool/population just as captive peregrines falcon's genes are buried in the wild population today. Captive bred birds are not wildlife as defined within the government codes. We should be a free enough society to dictate to our government what is rightfully our property.

Barn owls could be sold to each buyer of an owl nesting box to be raised and fledged from within that box. Later, when the owlet is flying free, the box could be mounted on a pole in the back yard or 'back forty" in a process falconers pioneered thousands of years ago called "hacking out," different from "hacking back" (to the wild).

This process is where food is offered in the nest box or below on the glove depending on the desired disposition outcome desired in the bird's psychology. In the box and the owl would be less tolerant of people later. Fed on the glove would be a human "imprint," making them tame for rearing in captivity for future breeding purposes and as a family pet.

Welfare organizations would spring from the well to care for injured and or orphaned barn owls. With annual events and bake sales that raise money for the charity. I am not selfish. I want to share the joy of keeping barn owls to the public worldwide.

Adult male barn owl proudly demonstrating at a bird show in Salt Lake City, Utah
Photo by Eric Peterson —Used with permission

Perhaps if each of us wrote letters demanding the de-regulation of barn owls and falcons and sent them to all our congressmen, to the president, to the US Department of the Interior, to the US Fish and Wildlife Agency and to the local news agencies, we could start this movement rolling.

The author at age three with his brother, Bob (rear), and his beloved rubber rooster at his nana's house in Youngstown Ohio. Circa 1956.
Photo provided by author

Chapter 14

Memories and Anecdotes

Some of my earliest memories are of a mobile that my grandmother sent to my mother. It hung over my bassinette and crib. It had vinyl blue jays and robins hanging from it. As an infant and young toddler I grabbed at them and chewed on them.

When I was about two years old, we flew back to Youngstown, Ohio where my grandparents lived. While we were there, Santa gave me a rubber rooster that "crowed" when I squeezed it. I fell in love with that silly rooster.

One can trace my fascination with birds and this book to the mobile and the rubber chicken. Raptor propagators and animal behaviorists call this "imprinting." From birth, I was "imprinted" with a love of all birds. I like to claim that the love of birds is in my DNA, but my early experiences only served to strengthen that love.

That love has opened many doors for me. I was fortunate enough to appear on a National Geographic TV program entitled *Terminal Velocity*. Later that same year, my peregrine falcon, Brooke, and I were featured on an Animal Planet show, also called *Terminal Velocity*. I've met some fascinating people and formed many wonderful memories. Many of those memories follow.

It Works!

Upon finishing an installation, I make it a habit to ask the client to call as soon as they see their first avian inhabitant inside the box. This keeps me informed of how my work is progressing and helps them to keep my card.

I received a call once from this suburban gent who explained that he got owls the first spring after I put up his nest box. However, he had lost my business card, in the interim. I had recently resumed my advertisement in his particular hometown newspaper after a five year absence. He explained over the phone that this was his first opportunity to phone me back.

As he was filling me in with the details such as "my wife just loves the baby owls" and the "rodents are not much of a problem anymore," I could hear shouting in the background. He asked me to hold the phone. Upon resuming the conversation, he explained that while we two were chatting, his wife had noticed a rat running along the top of their wooden fence.

They watched with great dismay as the rodent (Ratus ratus) jumped up to the service wire leading to their house. It had scurried most of the way up and was about to make good its escape when one of the barn owls appeared and snatched the rat deftly from the wire and was gone into the night.

He said that they threw their hands up and hugged each other.

Owlets In Situ

I had just replaced a ten year old nest box for a nice local couple. Upon completion they invited me into their posh home. This dwelling had recently been rebuilt after it had burned in a huge conflagration known infamously as the "Witch Fire."

In the vaulted great room a scorched and hollow but beautifully reworked oak tree trunk was wrapped by a beautiful staircase. At the 20' height of the stubs were owl droppings. I remarked that the tree must have been near the owl box prior to the couple bringing it inside for decoration. It looked to me that it must have been a fledging post at one point in time. This "post" is a tree, power pole or structure directly in front of the nest that they invariably try to fly to. They make their "maiden voyage" to this perch.

The hollow, scorched tree in the home rebuilt after the "Witch Fire."
Photo by Craig Hesse—Used with permission

The clients explained that it was decorated by the owls "in situ" or right where it was in the house.

Apparently during the reconstruction, the house was open framing. The oak tree trunk had been imported inside first and the framing built around it. When June rolled around, the owlets fledged as if on cue and flew from the box downhill to the top of the trunk. This is where they wait, or as I say 'set up station" and call for more rodents as the night passes.

The tree and the decorations provide "in situ" by the fledgling owlets.
Photo by Craig Hesse—Used with permission

As the work on the dwelling progressed, the sibling group, or "crèche," dispensed with the owl box altogether for the unfinished human habitat. The owls were seen perching daily in the rafters for the duration of building process and were frightened by the hammering and sawing not in the least.

When the framing and roof were on, a small hole was left under an eave so the owlets could continue to re-enter and exit the house. In time, one by one they dispersed to the four points and did not return.

The parent barn owls now enjoyed their well-deserved rest in the owl house. The clients cleaned up the droppings on the concrete floor prior to carpeting but decided to leave the adornments on the top of the trunk "for aesthetics."

The wood was prepared along the entire trunk with a polyurethane coating as a finish. The house keepers were not informed of this and were dismayed I am told because they were not able to scrub off the whitewash.

You Shyster

When I first began my installations, I never guaranteed that barn owls would control my clients' rodents, as there were no studies at that time that proved the efficacy of this rodent control method. Further, I never guaranteed the boxes would get an owl at all, let alone a breeding pair.

I did try my best with what knowledge I had then to place the box to attract owls. This was the position I took in 1992 when I began to create a market for nesting boxes. That policy remains as long as I do.

Having said that, I know of only two out of the almost

25,000 (and counting) boxes that I have personally installed that have never had an owl inhabit the box.

Well one of those finally did but it took 7 years. That box got a pair of owls breeding finally, but it had to be taken down not long thereafter due to wear and tear.

It was in a native American community way out in the countryside no less. Go figure.

The other was erected in the city of Pacific Beach, suburbia proper.

Murphy presided over this installation as well as this installation was for the secretary of the San Diego Audubon Society chapter. A lot was riding on this one. There were owls thereabouts in this neighborhood I knew so something was going on not apparent to my eye, like malicious people nearby perhaps. Maybe it was due to my old nemesis, rodenticides. I'll never know.

I did know there were owls in the area. When I am driving to a new area, I will stop at large fan palms here and there and walk around the trunk inspecting the ground for owl pellets.

Pacific Beach has barn owls. I know because I have put up a number of boxes there since and they all had owls to reside inside.

Some properties were just an absolute "lead pipe cinch" as my father would say. (This is one of his sayings from the toughest generation. He served as an ensign on a WW2 submarine.)

One of the first dozen boxes that I endeavored to install was for a nice lady and her husband who was less than nice. I rang the door bell and was "greeted" by a scowling man who summoned his wife. She however was all smiles and seemed very excited. Turns out this was a birthday present for her and she was glad to see my arrival.

Their house was atop a steep driveway with a grove of California Live Oak trees (*Quercus agrifolia*) opposite the home. She asked if it was possible for me to place the box somewhere so that she could see the owls in the box from her kitchen window.

I assured her that a tree was lending itself for just such a placement. As it indeed was.

She smiled and gave me the go ahead to install and retired to the house, leaving me alone with the husband, not a small man. As soon as his wife was no longer within earshot, this person stated that I was a "Shyster."

I begged his pardon and he repeated his conviction. A little louder the second time in case my hearing was not sufficient.

"You mean to tell me that an owl is going to go into that box?" he shot out.

Men are the more skeptical of the two genders I have found.

After I had just completed the "hang." This man repeated, closer this time, his brows depressing, "You are nothing but a shyster. BUT, its my wife's birthday and this is what she wants, so that's what she's going to get. Otherwise I'd run you off right now."

This was no doubt due to the fact that he now had to write the check for payment.

I am a veteran arborist and have had many a tree trimmer employee. The best and bravest climbers were quiet humble men. Guys, who if you ever did anger them, would somehow, be formidable opponents indeed. The "big talkers" were usually just that. Like this guy.

So I knew what to say to this man who was a doubting Thomas. I stated frankly but without confrontation that he was going to call me with an apology soon.

Two weeks passed and I got the call. To his credit he apologized to me and said that his wife was so very happy with her present as there was a new tenant residing inside the box.

One never knows if owls will reside in a newly installed box but I was really counting on one to show for this gentleman. The owl god had smiled, it seemed.

The Classes of Men

I have been told that, according to the theory of

"evolutionary psychology," which is the study of human actions today due to vestigial instincts from our clan past, there are two types of human male psychology— manipulators and agronomists.

Manipulators are the 'type A' personalities and follow after our hunting ancestors. They commute large distances to "make a killing' at the office, just like their hunting ancestors did. They manipulate their environment to suit their habitat needs. Like primitive man with fire or modern men with bulldozers and the like.

Agronomists like to plan for a harvest. They are the growers. Usually calmer and more understanding individuals.

I received a call from a client who was in distress. It seems that the young of a nest box had fledged prematurely.

It was a hot June day and my schedule was full. But due to the nature of my business and ethics involved, I made my way to his property to see if there was anything that I could do to help.

Upon arrival, I found owlets hiding here and there in the bushes in his back yard, about half a dozen total. Some where half grown and would not have left the box on their own accord that early, in my experience.

His wife was inside and not talking, as I assessed what I may do about the situation. She had been involved with the installation one year prior I recalled, but she was vacant from the scene this time.

What to do? How do I get the young back in the box without them immediately jumping back out as they panic when handled.

It seemed strange to me that all the owlets were on the ground at the same time. This is not the natural pattern of fledging.

Barn owls lay eggs every other day spread over an array of spring, not all at once like ducks or chickens. This is the "K and R" strategies as biologists term the way of laying and raising the "clutches" of eggs and chicks respectively. This optimizes the chicks survivability to coincide with the most favorable time of any given spring.

For example; if the mid spring was most favorable for the brood, bad weather subsiding for example, the chicks that were hatching during this time would be selected to survive better than those chicks that were laid prior to that period, maybe after as well.

Like a skipper of a submarine firing an array of torpedoes at a passing ship, one of them is bound to find its mark.

So the fledgling owlets are of ages grading from older to younger, first laid to last laid. Older owlets fledge first, then the next oldest and so forth. This was not the case here.

I took the pole and box down. I gently gathered the soft boned chicks and put them back in the box as the sun went down. As I had to re- erect the pole and box affair with the young inside, I wrapped a cord around a jacket and stuffed it in side the box, plugging the doorway. This so that after I erected the box, I could pull the cord and out would come the jacket, unplugging the doorway with the owlets inside. This way they would have an opportunity to settle down and not be inclined to immediately dive out of the box.

After erecting the nest box, I waited as long as I dared to pull the cord which yanked the jacket out of the doorway as the doorway was the birds only source air circulation. It had to be in place long enough for them to settle down, but not long enough to suffocate them. All went well.

I remained on the property, drinking some iced tea until it was dark enough for the parents to arrive for the chicks nightly feeding, which they did.

As I was about to leave, the husband suddenly went out to check on the young to see if they were still inside. Using a strong flashlight he approached the box and shined the light in side the nest box.

This action was unnecessary and was threatening to scare away the adult owls that were nearby. If the adults were to be frightened away, they could abandon their brood, undoing all the work I had just completed and putting the young in jeopardy .

I admonished him to vacate the back yard and for Pete's sake, turn that light off. This was when his wife told me that her husband had been shaking the pole that day "to make the babies fledge."

I was aghast. Some people lack common sense . I explained to him how things needed to go and left for home. Two days later there was an article in their local paper about the nest. This gentleman had called the paper to tout what a great job he had done to preserve the brood of young after their "mishap."

I build and install these boxes to the public with no small amount of reservation.

Learning One of Life's Lessons

In my home town, up on a cliff with a commanding view of the entire valley, is a golden eagle nest.

I'm one of those people that others often refer to as a "nature nut." I have an overwhelming need to see some wildlife every day. Without it, I feel incomplete. Each morning, I would make it a point to go past the cliff that holds the eagles' nest, or eyrie. With my nature fix fulfilled, I would go on to work at my tree service company. I love that nest. That I lived in a town that still retained what was special about it was my anchor.

One morning in 1991, I made a disturbing discovery. There, where there had previously been nothing but dark sage brush, I saw, in shocking brightness, a newly bulldozed road with many laterals. The main road went right up the

Golden Eagle Nesting in 2013 near Ramona, California.
Photo by John David Bittner—Courtesy of Wildlife Research Institute —Used with permission

side of the mountain to within 100 yards of the nest. A nest with an eaglet in it.

I felt so sorry for that poor little eaglet. Disturbed by the bulldozing work, the parents would not have returned to the nest to feed the eaglet while it continued. He probably had not eaten in at least two days. It was very possible that the parents had totally abandoned the nest and the eaglet. I was devastated. Although there were only a half dozen or so residents of the town knew of the nest or its inhabitants, we held it in enough esteem for the whole town.

A week later, I took my wife on a camping trip to one of my favorite areas. We went to Idaho where I had lived decades before. I was so disillusioned with what I saw as the lack of decency in our current state of residence that I hoped, by some long shot of luck, to persuade her to move to Idaho. My wife did like it there and we did move there, selling our home in the process. I didn't know it at the time, but this was the first step of the process that led to my almost complete financial and marital ruin.

My wife changed her mind about Idaho's residents. Two years later we were both back in San Diego. She had gone back to her mother's and had taken my only child, a daughter, with her. It took another year and a lot of effort, but we were able to reconcile and were reunited in a new home. Our ship of marriage had pulled off the reef with a new rising tide.

Through all of this I learned one of life's most important lessons. Do not run away from things that confront you. Stay and fight. So with my home life finally settled again, I decided to see what could be done about the development on the mountain. I went to the county permit office to see where this developer's project stood. I discovered that no permit was ever filed.

I pondered what to do. Soon I began my crusade. I began a letter writing campaign to any and all Government agencies, land trusts, Audubon Society and the Sierra club. Any time the County of San Diego Planning and Environmental review board held a meeting that had anything to do with this or any other project affecting eagles in San Diego County, I made sure I was there to speak. I would speak to anyone who would listen, Kiwanis,

Rotarians, garden clubs and school children.

I loved talking to the children. I remember clearly that at one school, the teacher had assembled two classes sitting about in a large circle. I had perched a hawk and a falcon there in the center of the grass and told them all about the illegal grading.

During this session with the children, a young boy asked if there were any eagles' nests near this school. Indeed there was. It had been abandoned a decade before because of the construction of the community we were now standing in. I didn't want to give away the location of the nest unless it was in jeopardy. I said, "Indeed, there is an eagles' nest so close to here, you wouldn't believe it," as I

Bald Eagles Nesting in 2013 within Ramona, California Grasslands Preserve.
Photo by John David Bittner—Courtesy of Wildlife Research Institute —Used with permission

glanced up at the long abandoned nest with its aging sticks on the mountain above.

As I did so, I noticed two large birds passing along the cliff face. They were the aging pair of golden eagles that used to nest at this site. They were now nesting on the back side of this mountain. As I continued speaking, keeping my eye on the birds, they flew out over the houses losing height until they were a mere 100 feet above our heads— directly over the children. They stopped their forward movement and began to circle and soar up slowly, the morning sun reflecting their golden crowns. They flew higher and higher until moments later, they were out of sight and gone. This experience was nothing short of magical.

I mentioned to the children that it might help if they would like to write letters to the county. I told them that I really hadn't gotten any help or cooperation from the "grown-ups" or any of the government agencies like the California Department of Fish and Game or the U.S. Fish and Wildlife Service.

These children did write letters to the County and to me, thanking me for my time. One child wrote "Money, Money, Money, is that all they ever think about?" and another who observed, "The land does not owe them a living." Such sage words. I still have the forty odd letters the children sent me and treasure them all.

Swinging Like a Pendulum

I once was looking for a Prairie Falcon eyrie in the Old Woman Mountains of California's Mojave desert. I was climbing up a lava trough that I call the "Hall of the Mountain Kings." It had hardened lava bubbles or "potholes" every few yards on the walls—an avian nesting gallery.

The falcons nest at the top, I was later to learn, and flew about the summit screaming their discontent at my presence as I dutifully checked each pothole on the way up. A barn owl was inadvertently flushed from a pothole and flew out into the broad daylight with a dry lake bed for a backdrop. I was marveling its beauty when it was suddenly and violently struck dead instantly by a

A natural barn owl nest site, cliffside near the surf in Del Mar, CA. This is similar to the nests in the lava potholes in the Old Woman Mountains
Photo by author

frustrated parent male Prairie Falcon. The falcon stooped from somewhere above and struck the owl in the head with a resounding WHACK. It fell lifeless on the sand hundreds of feet below. From then on I would do much more observing before I climbed the cliffs.

A couple of years later, about 1981, I climbed this same cliff face again and was successful at 'pulling" a young prairie falcon. I rappelled down but misjudged how much rope I had. With the fledgling in my shirt I hung at the end of my rope, as it were, outwards on an overhang about 45 feet off the steep boulder strewn rubble below. It was much too far to fall. I cursed myself for not bringing more rope or a friend and hung there most of the afternoon. Too tired to climb the skinny rope, I started to imagine the pile of bones that would greet some hiker years later as this area was many miles from the nearest paved road and truly remote.

I almost wore myself out trying to swing over to the cliff under hang but I could not come close to the wall. After what seemed an eternity, the wind began to blow. There was just slight breeze at first. Then it grew a little stronger. I began to gain a pendulum-like swinging. The wind grew stronger and in about another 45 minutes I was able to grab the cliff some 30 feet inwards. It was only after the wind aided me that I was able to finally grab a finger hold on the cliff face and try to find a way down.

I was, by no means, saved as I had to unclip from the safety line and climb down on the tiniest of bumps and little cracks with a very unhappy falcon in my breast. This was my only chance at salvation and I steeled myself to make it work.

I set little goals to achieve the big goals. (You see how falconry is a good life's teacher.) I told myself, "Just make that bigger bump 12 feet below without slipping. Ah! Great! Now to that little crack 7 feet down." I kept up this litany of self-encouragement until I reached the bottom of the cliff face. (I went back the following weekend to retrieve the rope I'd left hanging there.)

After I gained safety, I sat there exhausted but soon felt strangely invigorated. My stomach was all scratched up from the falcon inside my shirt (who I later named Glenda). She did not like me and even young prairies falcons are nasty tempered. But as I took in the magnificent view of the desert valley below, I knew that I was in heaven. Focusing on a dot below I realized that was my old Dodge truck (where I had some falcon food on ice) and I quickly snapped back to reality. If I didn't get a move on I knew I would navigating the washes and dunes in the dark. So I beat feet to my truck, where Glenda had her first meal as a falconer's charge. I then went to Landers, California and had a well deserved beer.

The Runaway

A contractor called me one day and told me he had installed an nest box on his property. This box was now old and falling apart, but it was full of baby owls. He hired me to put up a new box. As I installed the new box, the movement of the tree startled the owlets and one of the fledglings fled from the dilapidated box. This young female owlet glided down into the bushes. She began running away. If she had gotten lost, she could have been eaten by a coyote or a neighbors' dog.

My assistant was a large man, a Viet Nam vet. As far as I could see, he was not afraid of much of anything. He cornered the owlet.

"'Now what do I do?" he asked.

"I don't know, Don. Just don't let it get away!" I replied.

So he reached in the bushes and grabbed the owl. The owl grabbed back. I can still hear this macho man howl. He stood up and I saw that the owlet had clamped down on his hand. She was using her talons with her beak thrown in for good measure like some feathered crocodile. Soon, she was restored to her nest and peace reigned.

Backyard Barn Owls

My company was hired to trim and remove some trees at a lovely home and estate in Fallbrook, CA. I submitted a written proposal including the requested work. They noticed I had added the installation of a barn owl nesting box gratis. I explained what it was and the benefits of having sentry's guarding their property all night against invading rodents.

The homeowners were delighted and I dutifully installed

Backyard Barn Owls
Photo by Bert Kersey—Used with permission

one nest box, cleaned up the tree trimmings and collected a check. Two years later, my clients had a pair of barn owls inhabit the nest box. On a whim, Bert, the homeowner, began filming the owls and their antics. Soon he had so many excellent and interesting clips that he and his wife, Sharon, decided to produce a video about the owls.

This endeavor turned out to be a delightful video entitled *Back Yard Barn Owls*[1], winning two wildlife film awards. Burt and Sharon have gone on to produce another wonderful bird related video, Bring on the Birds! I

---

[1] This video and others are available at http://www.birdflix.com/pg1owlhome.html

realized once again that other people love what I love. That's a very gratifying feeling to this author.

Darwin Nods in Approval

My daughter's sixth grade teacher was one of those that truly appreciated wildlife. She put together a trip to the Galápagos Islands for my daughter's entire class and their parents. All the parents had to do was pay for it. We had bake sales and other fundraisers. I sold cords of Oak firewood at below market value and donated those funds to the cause. We did achieve our targeted fund amount and off we went, landing first in the delightful city of Quito, Ecuador.

Our next leg of the journey led to the Galápagos Islands, the archipelago made so famous by Charles Darwin. We had a wonderful time steaming around the islands in a little cruise liner, the Ambassador 2. During this cruise I turned 50 years old. These islands are sparsely populated except for the "Big Island" of San Cristobal. This entire voyage was charmed. The chain is a magic place. There I had an experience that was magical, like the eagles at the school.

The teacher arranged for our children to meet a class of Ecuadorian school children of similar age. During the socialization, my good friend Fred Sproul, botanist and biologist, suggested that I speak about barn owls. The Ecuadorian teacher there thought it was a good idea as well, but I was not so sure.

The kids assembled and I could tell not one of them

understood a single word I said about owls but I carried on. I was explaining what the owls looked like when suddenly a young boy who was seeking shelter from a light rain by moving under the eaves of the school suddenly spoke up and, in perfect English, said pointing, " Is that one right there?" We gathered around and to my surprise, there was a delightful adult male specimen of a Galápagos Island Barn Owl (*Tyto alba punctatissima*) perched above, roosting under the eave not 5 feet above us.

I noticed that this specimen was about half the size of the California Barn Owl (*Tyto Alba*) and he was colored darker, a sooty grey plumage morph to match the volcanic geology of the land. These changes were because of the isolation that the distance from the mainland gives this population of owls.

A Galápagos Island Barn Owl (Tyto alba punctatissima)
© Can Stock Photo Inc./pzurek—Used under license

I explained to the class that isolation brings mutations. Mutations bring change. Change brings new species. This is something I learned from Charles Darwin in his inspired book, *The Origin of Species*. Impulses ran up my neck and I looked around this beautiful place. I swear to you now, I could feel his hand upon my shoulder.

As I spoke I realized I had come an *Origin of Species* full circle without realizing it. I glanced at Fred and the teacher who had big grins showing. Somehow I knew that humble man who wrote this revelation of a book was nodding in approval.

Saving for a Box

I was contacted by Sara Rosenbaum, a teacher at the Scripps Ranch Montessori School. She said that she and her students had been saving where they could in the "garden budget" and a bit of their own pennies and dimes to purchase an owl box.

After months of saving, they had finally reached their goal to

The author installing a Hoo's HOO box at Scripps Ranch Montessori.
Photos by Sara Rosenbaum (Used with permission)

save enough to purchase and have installed one of my basic boxes ($350 installed).

When I was preparing to go to the school to install their basic box, I realized that I didn't have any Basics in stock. I found I was also fresh out of Ornate boxes as well.

As I thought about it, I decided that after all their hard work to save the money for a box, the kids really deserved to have a "Hoo's HOO" camera box. That way they could put the TV monitor in the science class room and observe the owls as they nested and raised their young.

I spoke to the children for a bit about owls and nature. They're all excited about having a box of their own and the possibility of having "their own" owls.

The author speaking to the students at Scripps Ranch Montessori.
Photo by Sara Rosenbaum (Used with permission)

Panic Averted

I recently received a rather urgent email from a client who was concerned because he feared the four owlets in his box had been abandoned. The mother, whom they called Shannon, had not returned to the box overnight and the owlets were alone.

He was assuming that this was due to the dense fog, injury or perhaps death. He wanted my advice on when he should call wildlife rescue to deal with the four owlets.

I immediately called him back and tried to reassure him that the female probably did not return to the box because of the unseasonal heat wave we were experiencing at the time. Judging by the photo of the owlets he sent me,

The four owlets—no apparent distress
Photo by Andrew Gepp—Used with permission

they did not appear to be any distress. I explained to him that one could read the comfort of chicks by their body language. Splayed out, they are too hot. Curled up, they are too cold. Slightly splayed with head up begging for food—just right.

I advised him to wait just a bit longer. I was pretty certain the mother was in a nearby tree watching over the box, but trying to stay cool and not heat up the box with her own body heat.

The next morning, I emailed him to check on the status of the owls in the box. He replied that yes, she had returned to the box overnight and was at that time in the box with the owlets. He said it had been an interesting night observing their behavior in the box. I can only imagine that the chicks were all glad to see their mother after not having her with them all day for the first time in their short lives. I also imagined that she must have been very anxious for the father, whom they called Seamus, to bring some prey items post haste.

Momma has returned!
Photo by Andrew Gepp—Used with permission

He and his wife assured me that the parents had brought in plenty of mice during the night and that the owlets seemed quite happy with full tummies.

At the time of this writing, all is well in that box. The parents are bringing in plenty of food, the owlets are thriving, and a panic response was averted.

Shannon gently nurturing her young ones
Photo by Andrew Gepp—Used with permission

An Evening Spent Owling

A client invited me to an "owling" at his house in San Clemente looking down on Nixon's "Western Whitehouse." He had three young owlets bouncing about the yard as they became more adventurous.

At first, they were walking about on the ground and making their way from one fledge spot to another. It was obvious that they had made extensive use of a large rock in the yard. They had adorned it with a lovely abstract painting decoration made from "liquid rats."

One of the main benefits of having an owl box installed, besides the obvious benefit of having a natural rodenticide, is the entertainment factor. It can be so engrossing to watch the young owlets get up the nerve to take the first step out of the box and then eventually venture forth to a nearby tree or fence post.

If you add floodlights to the yard a few weeks before the fledging, the owls get used to it and are not bothered by the lights when they do leave the box. The lights make it possible for you to see the owls and take wonderful photos as they cavort in your yard.

Above and facing page: An evening owling with the McPhee's in San Clemente, CA
Photos by the author

Barn owls will often return to a box year after year, providing both the service of keeping rodents in check and a nightly show full of laughter, thrills and even a few chills as they learn what they are capable of.

Some Rather Misguided Owl Box Designs

I got a call from a gentleman who wanted to hang his owl box. He had purchased one online. I had to tell him that unfortunately I wouldn't be able to hang it. It was HUGE,

A side-by-side comparison of a box purchased online and one of my ornate boxes.
Photo by author

heavy and very unwieldy. It had small openings near the top of the box, which meant it had to be taken down every year and cleaned out. This would be no small undertaking because of the size and weight of the box. I placed one of my ornate boxes beside it for comparison. I quickly realized that there really was no comparison at all—not in size, not in looks, not in practicality and not in appeal to owls or humans.

Once I got call from a gent who had a box that he had helped build. I get there and it was about four times the size of the box shown above. It was the size of a Volkswagen Beetle! It was so heavy I couldn't budge it and I am strong for my size. I bet it weighed four hundred pounds!

He asked if I could put it up in an oak tree. I gave him a look that meant "there's no way I am going to mess with it" and just said "How?" Then "Why?" as I gestured at my box on the ground next to his. I'll never understand the mindset that bigger must be better, especially when it comes to owl boxes.

There are many different individuals and companies online offering owl box plans or fully constructed owl boxes. Some may actually meet the requirements of the owls, but many do not. I urge potential owl box owners, whether they purchase from me or not, to take a close look at the box they are purchasing or building to determine whether it is sufficient to provide not only housing for its inhabitants, but also to provide protection, nurturing and a future for years to come.

It is sometimes a bit humorous to see how far some folks will go to make an owl box that doesn't really look like an owl box. Some boxes I have seen have been so elaborately decorated that they look more like they belong in a fantasy story or something.

It's very possible to make an owl box that is elaborate without going overboard. Some may want a box that reflects the design of their own home. Some may want a fairy tale castle. I've had one person request a box that looks like a Victorian home, complete with round turret and wide verandah.

The most elaborate owl box I've ever seen.
Photo by author

Variety is the spice of life as they say. Owl boxes do not have to be generic, cookie-cutter creations. It is important, however to make sure that , no matter the outside appearance, certain requirements must be met. These include: the correct size doorway, placed in such a way that the owl can remain unseen when desired; ventilation and or insulation to protect from hot summer days and cool spring or fall evenings; a doorway that is low enough that the owl can clean the box herself, eliminating the need for human intervention; outdoor surfaces and/or trees, fences and buildings close enough to provide plenty of branching opportunities for fledgling owlets; protection from predators with a pole that is high enough and sturdy enough and made of a material that doesn't allow predators to climb; and insect prevention, if necessary.

As long as those criteria are met, one can be as creative as desired with the exterior of the box. I'm sure many of my readers may come up with box designs of their own. I'd love to see designs by my readers.

So Many Memories

Over the last twenty years I've met so many different people as I've installed boxes. Some of these folks have been so very memorable, for both good and bad reasons. There's no way I could ever relate all the stories and memories I've collected. I've shared here, a variety of stories reflecting both the pleasant and unpleasant aspects of this business. I've been fortunate that the pleasant far outweighs the unpleasant. I wouldn't be doing this job if I didn't truly enjoy what I do. I'm nearing the milestone of 25,000 boxes installed. I hope there are at least another 50,000 to come.

A curios owlet checking out her "people"
Photo by Colleen Gepp—Used with permission

Afterwords

by

Bert Kersey

My wife Sharon and I first met Tom Stephan around 25 years ago when we desperately needed to diminish our new home's out-of-control gopher population. It was early January when Tom installed a plywood owl box in one of our big eucalyptus trees. He claimed we would probably have Barn Owls occupying the box within a few weeks — no guarantees of course (yeah, right). As I recall, it was only about ten days until we noticed a beautiful pair of owls setting up housekeeping in our brand new box. They acted every bit like they owned the place, and from that point on I guess they did.

The owl box wasn't close to our house so we almost forgot it was there. But we soon noticed some funky looking fuzzballs screeching their heads off in the doorway, and that's when the fun began — fun for us, not fun for the neighborhood rodents. Every night that spring, we watched both Barn Owl parents bringing in gopher after gopher and rat after rat. Our gopher population plummeted and we had a great time watching it all happen. Thanks for the fun, Tom!

We eventually moved across town and had Tom hoist another box into an oak tree outside our living room window. We eagerly anticipated the owls' arrival but this time it took almost three years for the first pair to move in. As an amateur video photographer, I couldn't resist setting up my camcorder and shooting what we saw going on just 60 feet away. What goes on in the dark of night is truly amazing!

Over the next two years I acquired umpteen hours of Barn Owl footage and turned it into a half hour "Backyard Barn Owls" video. We launched a "barnowls.com" website and Sharon and I started showing the video to garden clubs and Audubon groups around town, giving advice on attracting owls and building and installing owl boxes—the best advice being "call Tom Stephan."

A couple of years later I took my camcorder outdoors and shot another video, "Bring On the Birds," about the birds of the west — songbirds, water birds, hummingbirds, you name it. We are still showing both of our videos to bird fans of all stripes, and it all evolved from Tom's first owl box way back when.

People naturally have questions about Barn Owls and we tend to get the same ones over the years: How high should the box be? Which way should the doorway face? Should you clean out the box? But our all-time favorite came during a very serious phone call from a man with a very serious gopher problem: "Okay, I have lots of gophers and I constructed an owl box according to your plans. Now… where do I buy one of those Barn Owls?"

Sorry, even Tom can't help you there.

Technical Terms/Glossary

Arborist

A professional in the field of arboriculture. Involved in the management, cultivation, preservation and study of trees, shrubs, vines, and other perennial woody plants. An common, more informal term is 'Tree surgeon'.

American Kestrel

Falco sparverius. The smallest and most common falcon in North America. Sometimes informally known as the sparrow hawk.

Archeopteryx

A genus of early bird that is recognized as being the transition between feathered dinosaurs and modern birds. Sometimes known by the German name of Urvogel, or "original bird." From the ancient Greek ἀρχαῖος (archaīos) meaning "ancient," and πτέρυξ (ptéryx), meaning "feather" or "wing."

Bald Eagle

(*Haliaeetus leucocephalus*; *hali* = salt, *aeetus* = eagle, *leuco* = white, *cephalis* = head). A bird of prey found in North America. The national bird of the United States.

Although once endangered and on the brink of extinction, extensive conservation and preservation efforts have allowed the population to recover. Removed from the List of Endangered and Threatened Wildlife in the Lower 48 States on June 28, 2007.

Barn Owl

Tyto alba. The most widely distributed species of owl, and one of the most widespread of all birds.

Basal

Relating to the base or origin of a clade, or branch of animal or plant life. A clade consists of an ancestor and all its descendants. Preferred to the term "primitive"

Bipedal

An animal having two feet

California Condor Recovery Program

A conservation effort dedicated to restoring the population of the California Condor. http://cacondorconservation.org/programs/

Crepuscular

Active primarily during the twilight hours, primarily during dawn and dusk.

Cross-phase

Any two or more phases in a 3-phase electrical system making mechanical contact resulting in an immediate explosion with an arc flash and a complete meltdown of the conductors and equipment.

Darwin, Charles

(1809-1882) A British naturalist. Author of *The Origin of*

Species. Proposed the theory of natural selection.

Dimorphic

An observable difference between the two genders of a specific species. These differences may include ornamentation (coloring), size and behavior.

Dinosaur

A diverse group of animals of the clade Dinosauria. The word dinosaur means "terrible lizard," however, this is a misnomer, as dinosaurs are not lizards, but instead, represent a distinct group of reptiles.

Domestication

To train or adapt an animal to live in a human environment

Ducks Unlimited

An international nonprofit organization dedicated to the conservation of wetlands and associated upland habitats for waterfowl, other wildlife. http://www.ducks.org/

Dyonychus

A genus of carnivorous, bird-like, theropod dinosaurs that lived during the early Cretaceous Period, about 115–108 million years ago

Eagle Owl

The genus *Bubo*, primarily made up of the American (North and South America) horned owls and the Old World eagle-owls.

Eurasian Eagle Owl

Bubo bubo. A species of eagle owl resident in much of Eurasia

Falconry

The sport of hunting wild prey in its natural state and habitat by means of a trained bird of prey

Galápagos Island Barn Owl

Tyto alba punctatissima. Endemic to the Galápagos islands

Golden Eagle

Aquila chrysaetos. One of the best known birds of prey in the Northern Hemisphere. Present in Eurasia, North America, and parts of Africa

Great Horned Owl

Bubo virginianus. An eagle owl native to the Americas.

Imprint

Imprinting refers to a critical period of time early in an animal's life when it forms attachments and develops a concept of its own identity. Birds raised in captivity often imprint on their human caregiver. This makes it difficult, if not impossible, for the bird to set free to live on its own in the wild.

International Society of Arboriculture

An international organization promoting the professional practice of arboriculture and fostering a greater worldwide awareness of the benefits of trees. http://www.isa-arbor.com/about/index.aspx

Migratory Bird Treaty Act

A United States federal law, first enacted in 1916 in order to provide for the protection of migratory birds between the United States and Great Britain (acting on behalf of Canada). The act has since been expanded to include Mexico (1936), Japan (1972) and the Soviet Union (1976, now its successor state Russia).

Mutation

A relatively permanent change in hereditary material

National Audubon Society

A national organization dedicated to science, education and conservation, focusing on birds and other wildlife and their habitats. Named for John James Audubon (1785-1851), an American artist known for his brilliant paintings of the birds of North America. http://www.audubon.org/

North American Falconers Association

An association dedicated to the welfare of raptors in nature and in their careful employment in the sport of falconry. http://www.n-a-f-a.com/

The Origin of Species

A work of scientific literature by Charles Darwin, published in 1859. Considered to be the foundation of evolutionary biology. Its full title was *On the Origin of Species by Means of Natural Selection, or the Preservation of Favoured Races in the Struggle for Life*. For the sixth edition of 1872, the short title was changed to *The Origin of Species*.

Ornate Hawk Eagle

Spizaetus ornatus. A bird of prey from the tropical Americas. Like all eagles, it is in the family *Accipitridae*. This species is notable for its vivid colors.

Paleontology

The scientific study of prehistoric life

Peregrine Falcon

Falco peregrinus. Also known as the Peregrine, and

historically as the Duck Hawk in North America. A widespread bird of prey in the family Falconidae.

Peregrine Fund, The

A non-profit organization dedicated to saving birds of prey from extinction. http://www.peregrinefund.org/

Primitive

Earliest ancestor of a branch or plant life. The term "basal" is preferred as "primitive" may carry false connotations of inferiority or a lack of complexity.

Raptor

A bird of prey. Hunts for food primarily via flight, using their keen senses, especially vision.

Rodenticide

A category of pest control chemicals intended to kill rodents.

Strigiformes

In biological classification, the order containing owls. Two owl families are commonly recognized, the barn-owls (Tytonidae) and the typical-owls (Strigidae).

Tyto Alba

The Common Barn Owl

Tyto alba punctatissima

The Galápagos Island Barn Owl

Index

A-B	
Aerie (Eyrie)	140, 145
Air Superiority	xxi-xxii
Africanized Bee	43, 64
Albatross	13
American Kestrel	xxii, 100-105, 165, 178
Apatosaurus	i
Arboriculture	44, 165, 168
Arborist	44, 64, 67, 136, 165, 177, 178
Archeopteryx	6-7, 165
Audubon Society	3, 41, 134, 142, 169, 177
Backyard Barn Owls	148-149
Barbs	15
Barbulets	15
Basal	13, 166, 170
Basic Box	60, 152-153
Bee	42-44, 60, 63-64
Bipedal	1, 8, 17, 166
Bird Guard	98-99

C-E	
Calumus	34
Carson, Rachel	xi, xviii
Chain (for box installation)	45, 67
Cookie	26, 82-83
Crepuscular	66, 166
Crow	29-31, 39-41, 54, 62, 84

Curvaceous Feathers	7, 14, 26, 34
Darwin, Charles	8, 120, 150-152, 166, 169
Dinosaur	ix, 1-2, 6-8, 10, 24, 42 165, 167
Diurnal	15, 37, 61
Domestication	117, 123-127, 167
Double Clutch	80
Down	7, 14, 26-27, 35-36, 88, 94
Duplex Box	55, 76
Dyonychus	8, 167
Eagle Owl	3, 30, 95, 167, 168
Eurasian Eagle Owl	95, 167
Eyrie (Aerie)	140, 145

F-H

Falconry	v, 9-10, 25, 87-88, 96, 104, 113-114, 117, 147, 168, 169
Faure, Austin	xv, xxv, 50
Finley, W.L.	4
Fir Out	61-62
Fledging	x, 24, 27, 28, 31-34, 52, 53, 57, 62, 68, 126, 131-132, 137-138, 140, 156-157
Galápagos Islands	14, 150-151, 168, 170
Golden Eagle	ix, 6, 9, 92, 94, 98, 104, 114, 140-141, 168, 176, 180
Gopher	ix, 19-20, 25, 33, 86, 125
Great Horned Owl	3, 29, 30, 167, 168
Gyrfalcon	26, 35, 113-115, 125
Hawaiian Tern	73
Hawking	iv, v, vi, 40, 113, 176, 185
His and Hers Box	55, 76
Hoo's HOO Box	48, 49, 152-153
Huxley, Thomas	8

INDEX

I-O

Imprinting	122, 127, 129, 168
Kestrel	xxii, 100-105, 165, 178
Killer Bee	43, 64
Lee, General Robert E.	39
Liquid Rats	20, 89, 156
Loft	35
McGee	iv, xviii, xxiv, 22, 49-56
Migration	14, 37, 75, 114, 116, 179
Migratory Bird Treaty Act	98, 113-117, 168
Molly	xx, xxiv-xxv, 19, 22, 23, 31, 49-56
Molt	26-27, 34-37
National Audubon Society	3, 41, 134, 142, 169, 177
Origin Of Species, The	8, 151-152, 168, 169
Ornate Box	41, 58, 62, 80, 153, 158
Ornate Hawk Eagle	62-63, 169
Orphaned Owlets	119-121, 127
Ostrum, John	8

P-R

Paddling	26, 28
Palm	53-54, 58, 108, 134
Peregrine	x, 3, 15, 17, 18, 24, 74, 75, 114, 116, 126, 129, 169, 170
Peregrine Fund, The	v, 75, 170
Plumage	vi, 14-16, 26, 34-39, 101, 151
Poison	xi, xxv, 56, 71, 74, 107-111, 118
Pole (for box installation)	xxii-xxiii, 20, 22, 28, 41, 46-47, 55, 61, 70, 126, 138-139, 160
Preening	36
Primary Feathers	17

Primitive	13, 166, 170
Puffy	92-97
Pygostyle	36
Rachis	15
Ramona Airport Field	179-181
Ramona Grassland	xviii, 112, 141, 143, 176, 179-181
Rat	19, 20, 25, 33, 56, 72-74, 84, 87, 89, 107-108, 124-125, 130, 156
Rodent	x, xiii, xix, xxv, 16, 19, 25, 32, 33, 37, 51, 53, 65, 66, 70, 71, 73, 74, 76, 81, 84, 85, 86-87, 88, 101, 102, 104, 107-111, 116, 124, 125, 130, 132, 133, 148, 157, 170, 178
Rodenticide	xi, xiii, 56, 74, 107-111, 134, 156, 170
Rowing	26-27
Royal, Carlos	xv, xxi-xxv, 20, 49-55
Royal, Donna	xv, xxi-xxv, 49

S-Z

Screech Owl	105
Secondary Feathers	36
Sevin Dust	43, 63
Strigidae	170
Strigiformes	1, 13, 170
Tern	73
Theropod	1, 16, 167,
Transformer	91
Tridactyl	16
Tyrannosaurus Rex	1, 26

Tyto	14, 15, 74, 151, 166, 168, 170
Tyto Alba Punctatissima	151, 168, 170
Uropygial Gland	36
Ustream.tv	xxv
US Fish And Wildlife Service	98, 127
Velociraptor	1, 3, 8
Wandering Albatross	13
Wildlife Research Institute	ix, 178
Windle, Rick	xv, 49
Witch Fire	98, 131
Zygodactyl	16

Contemplating that first step out of the box
Photo by Colleen Gepp—Used with permission

Author hawking rabbits with Goshawk on land near the Ramona Grasslands Preserve. This land was recently approved by the San Diego County Board of Supervisors for housing development. It is prime Golden Eagle habitat as the birds perch there daily to hunt.

About the Author

Tom Stephan is a certified arborist, a tree trimmer and an avowed lover of raptors and birds in general. It seems that he comes by his love of birds naturally. It's in his genes. A paternal ancestor, Count Heinrich von Stephan, was a falconer in Prussia. His grandmother worked diligently to restore the presence of bluebirds in her Ohio neighborhood. Not only were her efforts wildly successful, but she soon became president of her local Audubon Society chapter. She went on to be the awards chair for the National Council of Garden Clubs of America.

As a child, inspired by her devotion to avian wildlife, Tom soon learned to identify the birds that lived in the many canyons in and around La Jolla Shores, California.

When Tom was in second grade, a school research report led him to a 1940s National Geographic article about naturalists/biologists, John and Jean Craighead. Their story captivated him. He was soon a daily regular at the local pet shop. Tom's first raptor was a kestrel given to him by the owners of that pet store, creating in him a life-long enthusiasm (some would say obsession) for raptors. His friendship with his kestrel led him to an avid quest for other birds of prey to observe in

Tom often provides educational programs about raptors, conservation, rodent control and wildlife preservation to groups around the area.

their natural habitat. By the time Tom reached his teen years he was an agile tree climber, scaling every tree he could find that might contain an eagle, hawk or owl nest. The knowledge and skills he obtained from this activity naturally led to work as a tree trimmer. He later was certified as an arborist. As he worked as a tree trimmer, Tom began installing owl nest boxes. Over the last 20 years he has installed almost 25,000 boxes!

Tom is a Master Falconer, a title that is not taken lightly, nor easily attained. It involves years of apprenticeship, training, testing and experience. Years ago, Tom's work with raptors was noted by a local reporter who asked him to serve as a guide to a group of nature enthusiasts who wanted to explore the canyons. It still gives Tom great pleasure to serve as a guide to naturalists and nature lovers, taking them into the more wild, often unseen areas and sharing with them his passion, knowledge, and reverence of nature.

In the late 1980s, Tom found that the entire 4,000 acres of the Ramona Airport Field, home to an immature, female bald eagle and other wildlife, was destined to become a new development – a city to be. The loss of this habitat would have been devastating. It was the densest population of native and migrating raptors in San Diego County and, possibly anywhere in Southern California. Tom was determined to do what he could to save this natural habitat. He was responsible for the founding of the Ramona Hawk

The Ramona Airport Field, now the Ramona Grasslands Preserve.
Photo by Craig Hesse—Used with permission

The Ramona Airport Field, now the Ramona Grasslands Preserve.
Photo by Craig Hesse—Used with permission

Watch, an effort to educate others about nature and raptors and to save the Ramona Airport Field.

Soon, David Bittner, a raptor biologist, founded the Wildlife Research Institute (http://www.wildlife-research.org/) near the Ramona Airport Field. It was called the Grasslands Headquarters office. The WRI now has some eight staff members doing golden eagle and other raptor studies all over the west. Bittner got the Nature Conservancy to purchase most the land with additional money from local governments. The field and its inhabitants have been saved. Presently, another new young female bald eagle is nesting on those grounds, just 20 miles away from the major metropolis of San Diego.

Tom is grateful that his passionate hobby has led him to such a fulfilling career. He spends his days sharing his enthusiasm

ABOUT THE AUTHOR

and knowledge of nature and its inhabitants with people around the world.

That is his definition of success.

Wildlife Research Institute Grassland Headquarters in the Ramona Grasslands Preserve
Photo by Craig Hesse—Used with permission

A chain-hung Basic box blends into the landscape surrounding it.
Photo by author

Photo and Illustration Credits

Baden-Baden Kur & Tourismus	10
Katherine Bannister	77
John David Bittner	141, 143
Les Blenkhorn	96
Becky Boberg	115
Steve Chindgren	123, 124, 127
Stephen Ford (Stephen Ford Photography)	116
Bob Franz	xxvi, 33
Andrew Gepp	52, 154, 155
Colleen Gepp	viii, xii, xiv, xvi, 12, 21, 105, 110, 120, 162, 175
Charles Gilband	122
Lauren Greider	67, 69
Craig Hesse	38, 40, 45, 70, 78, 82, 83, 94, 100, 103 104, 112, 118, 131,132, 178, 179, 181
Bert Kersey	109, 149
Joshua Myers	9, 185
Sara Rosenbaum	48, 152, 153
Carlos Royal	xviii, xx 23, 26, 28, 33, 50, 51, 53, 54, 56, front cover
Donna Royal	23
Peter Schouten	7
Doug Sooley	60
Tom Stephan	55, 74, 80, 89, 90, 91,93,95 98, 108, 119, 138, 145 158, 160, 182, back cover
Robert Weigand	49
Wildlife Research Institute	141, 143
With license from CanStock Photo	29, 30, 73, 111, 151

Contact Information

Tom Stephan
tom@air-superiority.com
www.barnowlboxes.com
(760) 789-1493   Cell (760) 445- 2023

Dorothy D. Lafferty
Dorothy Lafferty has always been an avid reader and student of the world around her. After retiring from service in Public Health, she devoted her time to her husband and special needs daughter. She has written and illustrated four children's story books and compiled over 50 cookbooks and reunion directories for individuals and organizations.

SonShine Creations—http://chatterchopz.com
sonshinecrtns@chatterchopz.com

Chris Meador
Chris Meador's interest and research on Golden Eagles and other raptors started when he was only twelve. He is currently the Assistant Director of the Wildlife Research Institute and has dedicated his life to wildlife research, public education and habitat conservation.

http://www.wildlife-research.org/
cmeador@wildlife-research.org

Carlos Royal
Carlos Royal is a retired real-estate guru who now enjoys travel and observing and celebrating in the world around him. He has published two books of photography detailing the lives of Molly and McGee, the world's most famous barn owls.

cwroyal@cox.net
www.carlosroyal.com
http://mollysbox.wordpress.com/blog/

CONTACT INFORMATION

Craig Hesse

Craig Hesse has enjoyed the challenges and successes of wildlife photography for many years. Raised in the snow-belt of western New York state, he attended Genesee Community College and Erie Community College after serving in the U.S. Navy in 1967-1971. After spending the last 23 years in the photo-finishing industry he now enjoys concentrating his time on wildlife, scenic, and the world of macro-photography. Married for more than 30 years to the love of his life, Cheryl, a passionate equine trails enthusiast. They have one daughter Megan, an in-demand portrait photographer in her own right. Craig is the grandfather of Tyler, a student in Baldwin-Wallace University, and a beautiful new granddaughter, a red headed baby girl, Fiona. CraigHesseImages@gmail.com.

Photo by Craig Hesse
Used with permission

Bert Kersey

Bert Kersey is an avid birdwatcher and photographer. For him, the big benefit of bird photography — besides keeping his life list honest — is that he can, in effect, "capture" and bring home the birds that he sees, and study them for details and ID clues. He has very effectively done this in his two videos, *Backyard Barn Owls* and *Bring on the Birds*.

http://www.barnowls.com
contact@barnowls.com

Headed home after a Sunday's hawking.
Photo by Joshua Myers—Used with permission

Made in the USA
Charleston, SC
23 September 2013